Reclaiming Social Work:
The Southport Papers
Volume Two

Edited by
Ian Paylor, Jennifer Harris,
and Lynn Froggett

VENTURE PRESS

BASW website: http://www.basw.co.uk

Published by
VENTURE PRESS
16 Kent Street
Birmingham
B5 6RD

British Library Cataloguing-in-Publication Data
A catalogue record for this book is available from the British Library

ISBN   1 86178 046 X   (paperback)

Cover design by:
Western Arts
194 Goswell Road
London
EC1V 7DT

Printed in Great Britain

Contents   Page

Chapter 9
Community Care, Community Work
                    and Social Exclusion   **99**
Peter Sharkey

Chapter 10
Children and Families Social Work
                    – Visions of the Future   **113**
Annie Huntington

Notes on Contributors

Cathy Aymer is Director of Professional Studies in the Department of Social Work at the University of Brunel. After several years working with children in residential care she still maintains her interest in residential institutions and children on the margins. Her other research interests are in the experiences of black students in higher education and black professionals in white welfare organisations.

Julian Buchanan worked for many years as a probation officer and later manager with the Merseyside Probation Service. He has particular interest in issues of social exclusion, problem drug-use, and probation training and social work education and has published widely. Currently he is a senior lecturer at the University of Central Lancashire and Course Leader for the MA in Substance Misuse.

Derek Clifford has had an interest in assessment in social work for many years, as a practitioner mainly in child care in Manchester and Stockport, and as a Senior Lecturer in Social Work at Liverpool John Moores University. He has also had a long-standing interest in theory and values in social science since being a lecturer in political theory in Trinidad and Australia, and through experiencing different cultures and parenting two daughters. He is the author of a number of papers on assessment, and a book: Social Assessment Theory and Practice, Ashgate, 1998.

Lynn Froggett has a practice background in child care and mental health. Her current academic interest is in the application of psychoanalytic social theory to the understanding of social work policy and practice.

Dr. Jennifer Harris BA (Hons) CQSW, is a Senior Research Fellow in the Social Policy Research Unit, University of York. Her first book, The Cultural Meaning of Deafness was published by Avebury Press (1995) and her second Deafness and the Hearing by Venture Press (1997). Her research interests are in the fields of qualitative methodology, and disability studies and outcomes for service users and carers.

Dr. Annie Huntington is currently employed as lecturer in the Department of Social Work at Salford University. Prior to this she worked as a children and families social worker in the statutory and voluntary sector, a general nurse, a prison tutor, and lecturer in the further education sector. More recently she has trained and qualified as a psychodrama psychotherapist. She has published in a number of journals including Practice, Child and Family Social Work, Groupwork, and the British Journal of Psychodrama and Sociodrama.

i

Malcolm Millar was a probation officer in Bristol for several years. Since 1990 he has been a lecturer in Social Work Studies at Liverpool University. He has published in the fields of psychology and social work, child protection work, probation practice, and social work education. Currently, his research is particularly concerned with the problematic interface between the complex dilemmas of day-to-day social work practice and the prescriptions offered by social work 'theory' of various types.

Mike Nellis is involved in the training of probation officers in the Midlands region. His current interest is in penal policy, particularly restorative justice and electronic tagging, and the emerging concept of 'Community Justice'.

Toyin Okitikpi is a lecturer and course leader for the BA (Social Work) programme at the University of Brunel. Prior to joining Brunel he worked for many years in local authorities with children and families. He has a strong interest in comparative studies in different EU countries about their responses to refugee children. He has researched mixed-race relationships and written about mixed-race children.

Ian Paylor is a lecturer in Applied Social Science at Lancaster University. His current research and teaching interest is in the areas of young offenders and social work with drug users. Previous research has concerned local crime surveys; an evaluation of a project designed to assist unemployed young males; evaluation of youth workers' practice; provision of legal services; evaluation of change within a social service department; the needs and problems of seasonal workers; social work with young offenders; assessing older adults' numerical skills; understanding change in a family centre; the experiences of men and women leaving prison; and job satisfaction and dissatisfaction amongst residential care workers

Jackie Powell is a Senior Lecturer in the Department of Social Work Studies at the University of Southampton. She has worked in a number of practice settings and has carried out research in various organisational settings. Her main research and teaching interests include evaluative research methodologies and the impact of changing policy and organisational structure on patterns of service provision and professional practice. She is currently involved in several research projects which are exploring inter-agency and inter-professional working at the health and social care interface.

Peter Sharkey has been a social worker and a community worker in Liverpool. He is currently a Principal Lecturer in the School of Law & Applied Social Studies at Liverpool John Moores University and is course leader for the degree in Applied Social Studies. Publications include Introducing Community Care, 1995, Collins Educational, and The Essentials of Community Care, 2000, Macmillan. He has also written 10 open learning workbooks on community care published by the Open Learning Foundation and BASW.

John Stewart is a senior lecturer in social policy in the Applied Social Science Department at Lancaster University, where he has been teaching and researching for 25 years. He has written extensively on the relationship between the material deprivation of individuals and families and social service provision. Current research is on wheelchair users and housing issues, and the Labour Government's new deals as part of its welfare-to-work project.

Chapter 1
Making a Difference
Ian Paylor, Jennifer Harris, and Lynn Froggett

The aim of this introduction is twofold: first, to tell the story of the conference from which the chapters which form this book were drawn, and second,
to describe the contribution each of them makes within the overall conceptual scheme for the book.

The conference, *Social Work, Making a Difference?* held in Southport in
March 1999, was the brainchild of Bob Sapey and he remained the driving
force behind the enterprise. A steering committee comprising the editors of
this book, plus Julian Buchanan, John Washington, Francis Young and a fluc-
tuating collection of colleagues from the University of Central Lancashire's
Department of Social Work, and the British Association of Social Workers
(BASW) was established and worked tirelessly at the tasks involved in
putting together an international conference from scratch.

In conceiving the event as our department's modest contribution to the
process of millennial reckoning, we wanted to make sure that it was broadly
based and had an identity that we could own. Discussions around the choice
of name and referees helped us to clarify our ideas on this. We had been
guided by a desire to ensure high standards while maintaining a critical and
imaginative stance. Our original intention had been to call the event *What
Works in Social Work?* but Audrey Mullender pointed out that this carried
connotations which could easily align us with the discourse of effectivity
represented by the growing evidence-based practice movement. While we
were concerned to see diversifying forms of evaluation in the welfare field,
and hoped that they would be represented at the conference, we were alarmed
at the resurgence of positivist methodologies. These are clearly attracting
considerable support and funding at the present time. They are congruent
with a technical-rational managerialism which arguably threatens the value-
base of social work and its interpersonal grounding, and poses serious
challenges for those among us who wish to develop alternatives that we
would consider to be more appropriate to a reflective and critical practice.

Our choice of papers for the conference reflected these concerns and revealed a
consistency of approach between ourselves and the referees. It also led to more
than one argument with potential contributors who felt that they should not
have been excluded. While we acknowledged that a case could be made for

'fighting it out' we were concerned that the conference could be used as a thinking space rather than an adversarial forum. There were after all other cross-currents and conflicting agendas.

This book is made up of a collection of papers from the conference. All the abstracts submitted for consideration as part of the conference programme were reviewed by our team of referees, Professor Audrey Mullender, University of Warwick; Professor David Smith, University of Lancaster, and Professor Chris Jones, University of Liverpool. In the end, there were over 100 papers presented at the conference plus nine keynote speakers.

Putting together the papers for this edited collection was a task undertaken by the editors over a 12-month period. An early decision was that the papers which make up the volume should not be restricted to the keynote speakers. Following this decision, the book and the work involved in its production took on their own momentum. In the usual way, all conference contributors who were to attend to give their papers were invited to write a full paper for consideration by the editors.

Reviewing all the submissions was a mammoth task and we were impressed with their exceptionally high quality. We finally devised a 'scoring' system and those papers which appear in this volume basically got the highest scores! As well as assessing the papers for the obvious features such as the quality of the writing, the depth of analysis, and coherence of the argument we were also looking for work that engaged us, questioned us, and intrigued and intellectually entertained us. Following this process we had 25 papers of high quality from which to select 9 or 10 for each volume of the book. The final selection process proved very difficult indeed. Were it not for the deadlines we would probably still be debating the decisions. The final product, we feel, reflects the major issues raised at the conference and also contributes to the ongoing debates within the social work press.

The collection
We begin with Lynn Froggett's unusual article which is a critical, sometimes whimsical, and ultimately upbeat reflection on the current vogue for using the promotional techniques of commercial organisations to 'sell' change within social services departments. Drawing on a study of a particular agency she explores the ways in which these can backfire producing resistance or cynical withdrawal among the very staff they are designed to convince. She argues that processes of transformation in the field of human welfare raise aspirations to trust and authenticity which can be jeopardised

by promotional techniques. She identifies in the use of narrative an aesthetic sensibility which is more appropriate to the nature of care.

In a contrasting but complementary chapter Julian Buchanan and Malcolm Millar argue that several processes have combined to threaten and virtually overwhelm the identity of state social work in Britain. These include government responses to child abuse enquiries, the growing emphasis upon competence in social work education, and the dominance of conceptions of individual responsibility within a market economy. They argue that social work's resistance to such pressures has too often been politically naïve and intellectually limited. In particular, counter arguments which have relied heavily upon ideas of empowerment, partnership, and anti-oppressive practice have frequently been presented in a way that obscures the complex identity of social work with its tension between care and control, and its consideration of personal responsibility as well as individual rights. Whilst there is much in the recent changes to the Probation Service to criticise, Buchanan and Millar suggest that social work can learn from the way in which the probation practice has traditionally balanced care and control, using knowledge and social work values to underpin its work with clients. Taking examples from probation practice with drug users, they offer an analysis of social work which explicitly incorporates the need for care and control. In the present political climate it may be difficult to reverse the restructuring of social work with its growing emphasis upon regulation and social control. However, they argue that a simplistic promotion of empowerment has done the profession no favours and it is vital that the complexity of social work can be communicated effectively.

In a similar vein Mike Nellis's chapter seeks to question the concept of oppression as it has been used hitherto in the literature on social work values, and in the practice of social workers and probation officers. He asks why the idea of oppression has been applied exclusively to issues of race, gender, age and disability, and sexuality, and why contemporary social work has failed to acknowledge that the managerial practices with which it is now so thoroughly infused are sufficiently corrosive of personal autonomy to count as a form of oppression in their own right. He suggests that there is within the social work and probation worlds a 'deliberation deficit' in respect of these issues, for which the university departments which train social workers and probation officers are at least as responsible as the agencies and the Government, who have been pressing for even more vocational – and *potentially* anti-intellectual – forms of training.

Against the backdrop of an unprecedented growth in evaluation and successive governments' attempts to control public expenditure and implant a new managerial culture in the public sector, Jackie Powell argues that evaluation has been presented as a prerequisite of effective accountability and significant change. Accountability, however, states Powell, is a problematic concept. The reconciliation of the individual's needs for accessible and responsive service represents a major challenge for those engaged in researching and evaluating the implementation of current policies espousing principles of social inclusion and controlled public expenditure. Focusing on issues of accountability in the context of implementing community care policies, Powell explores some mechanisms for encouraging participation and debate between a range of different parties, including some not previously involved in the process of service planning and delivery. In doing so, she raises underlying issues relating to the problematics of communication and knowledge, claims and argues the need for an approach to evaluation which involves people in dialogue and debate directed towards shared understanding as a basis for change.

Derek Clifford's chapter *Revaluing Professional Social Work Assessment* offers a theoretical framework which has been tested and supported in practice settings. He relies on perspectives from feminist and disability research and suggests the use of a critical autobiographical framework which can incorporate understanding derived from the life experience of the assessor. The approach rests on both social and psychological concepts and a number of key principles informed by anti-oppressive, political and ethical commitments. These draw strength and credibility from their grounding in the best traditions of existing social work practice.

In *Action for Inclusion* Cathy Aymer and Toyin Okitikpi are concerned with the predicament of refugee children from African countries. These young people are arriving in Britain in the context of rising numbers of asylum-seekers and an international clamp-down on migration from developing countries. Frequently they have experienced unimaginable levels of trauma, dislocation and loss which threaten the very possibility of an integrated self. The research carried out by these authors has demonstrated the inconsistent and fragmented nature of response to these children. Whereas immediate material needs for shelter are dealt with well, there are no guidelines for comprehensive assessment, and attention to long-term well-being is at best haphazard. They argue for a 'joined-up' approach in which short-termism can be avoided and health, education, and therapeutic needs can be coherently addressed.

In their chapter Jennifer Harris and John Stewart discuss the nature of the relationship that disabled people have with the welfare state. The modern disability movement has pursued a rights approach to benefits and services in order to achieve the inclusion of disabled people in mainstream society. Considerable gains have been made through these strategies in the area of income maintenance and welfare rights. Exercising these rights has become problematic because disabled people have started to be viewed as part of the 'underclass' and because they have had to trade their 'deserving' privileged and quasi-charitable status for rights and entitlements. Disabled people must now compete with all the other groups seeking more-equitable treatment over income maintenance. Nowhere are these tensions between a rights and a needs approach more apparent than in the provision of 'special needs' housing. Harris and Stewart argue that in the process of struggling to claim their rights to benefits and services, disabled people have become enmeshed in a dependency relationship with the welfare state. The role of the professional has been one of dependency creation – characterised by paternalism and expert determinism of social need.

Peter Sharkey's chapter on *Community Care, Community Work, and Social Exclusion* points to the individualisation of responses to social need following the introduction of the Community Care legislation in the early 1990s. He suggests that social services departments are being largely bypassed in government initiatives aimed at community regeneration. Community work techniques which aim to develop and sustain active social support networks have much to offer. In particular, they can help to refocus attention on the structural causes of poverty and disadvantage while linking it with other dimensions of social exclusion.

In the concluding chapter of the book, Annie Huntington explores a number of interrelated themes focused on the nature and future of social work with children and families, within statutory social work agencies. More specifically she explores the extent to which the debate around the balance between child protection and family support services has been structured to meet ideological and political ends, linked to particular conceptions of value for money and the relationship between the child, family, and state. Whether social workers, employed within statutory agencies, have a future role either in terms of providing supportive interventions or fulfilling protective functions is, she argues, debatable. The face of social work is changing and it is possible, she argues, that shifts which may have previously seemed unimaginable are rapidly becoming a reality.

Conclusion

Looking back, we were clear that the main purpose of the conference was to examine the potential of social work to make a difference in the lives of marginalised populations who are becoming ever more vulnerable at a time of momentous economic, social, and cultural change. These changes – globalisation, altered patterns of poverty and social exclusion, and the misfit between single-issue and identity politics and collectivist welfare provision – inevitably provided the backcloth against which our discussions took place. Our four main themes were social and policy change, knowledge and ethics, communication imagery and ideology, research and evaluation. These lent themselves well to contextualisation and the linking of very diverse issues which proved enormously productive and gave depth to our deliberations, allowing themes to re-emerge in successive papers, and to be developed throughout the course of the proceedings. Some of us had been concerned that the economics of a large international conference seemed to dictate a post-modern model (in the worst sense): a blizzard of short, disconnected papers with no apparent relation to each other – each one entertaining enough in its own right, but leaving the impression of pastiche rather than emergent narrative. One comes away with the impression of a process driven by participants' institutional obligations to meet their performance indicators rather than engage in dialogue.

Apart from the fact that we felt that these exercises are intellectually futile, there was an impelling reason to avoid such a pitfall. Social work is far too important in the lives of disadvantaged people to waste time in this way and the task of forging links between academics and practitioners too urgent and too difficult to lose a valuable opportunity. It seems to get progressively more difficult to create venues for discussion in which both are represented – particularly when they concern the larger themes that impact on the profession. It has been observed often enough that this has impoverished our debate and weakened our research base. The project of holding the conference in conjunction with BASW was intended to help us bridge this divide. In the end we cannot honestly claim that we were able to achieve the kind of balance we had hoped for. Academics are of course more likely to be financially supported by their organisations for such events and they outnumbered practitioners and managers. Nevertheless the influence of the latter is palpable in both the keynote speeches and the subsequent papers and helped us to justify our conference title: *Making a Difference.* Social work *has* historically made a difference to millions of people who would otherwise have suffered the effects of poverty, poor housing, social exclusion, and prejudice. It will clearly continue to change, but we may rest assured that social problems and inequalities will persist and require our attention.

Chapter 2
Care and Commodity Aesthetics: Fetishism and transformation in social welfare.

Lynn Froggett

This chapter draws on a study of policy implementation in a social services department to investigate the effects of an emphasis on presentation as a means of promoting and sustaining change. It examines ways in which a particular object – a specially designed plastic folder – was invested with a symbolic significance reflective of the impact of wider cultural anxieties about social welfare[1]. It discusses the contradictory character of the folder as a vehicle for transformational aspirations and suggests that it was unable to perform this function adequately because it introduced a commodity aesthetic which staff perceived as inappropriate within their field. Finally, it draws attention to the emergence of a narrative sensibility as a result of revitalised communicative relationships and suggests that this provided a more acceptable basis for organisational change.

The research that stimulated this paper started off as a reasonably straightforward evaluation of a supervision policy in a social services department. The straightforward report of the results has been published elsewhere (Froggett, 1999a) and will not be my main concern here. As it turned out there was nothing at all straightforward about the way in which the policy was conceived, or perceived or received. Some of the complexities arose from the attempt to initiate a process of cultural change which would counter what management regarded as an outmoded dependency culture among certain sections of the organisation. This is a theme of some interest since the notion of dependency culture derives from the neo-liberal discourse of the entrepreneurial self: individualistic, autonomous, competitive, self-interested, and motivated by material success. The Labour Government appears to have taken over this heritage albeit with a 'new' or 'modern' inflection. It is questionable whether such attributes find satisfactory expression in welfare work or in welfare organisations and in an earlier paper (Froggett, 1999b) I analysed the contradictions between attempting to establish a reparative and developmental culture and over-valorising the qualities extolled by business and commerce.

My aim here is to pick up on another related theme which was raised in the course of the study – namely the effect of what for want of a more elegant term I shall call 'presentationalism'. I see this as linked to a commodity aesthetic which is pervasive within consumerist societies and has increasingly extended into the field of social care. By presentationalism I mean the assumption that the key to rendering a measure acceptable or desirable lies in the manner in which it is introduced or 'sold' to the people affected by it, rather than in its intrinsic worth. The problem with such an assumption lies in the extent to which it promotes attempts to administer the production of trust, thereby unwittingly undermining it. In British politics it was Margaret Thatcher who made the decisive leap in electoral technique from persuasion to presentation. The employment of a leading advertising agency to make-over the persona of the party and its leader incorporated the technologies of public relations and commercial promotion into the political process to an extent previously witnessed only in the United States. In this respect, as in others, New Labour has surpassed the initiatives of its predecessors. Public anxieties about these developments seem to revolve around the issue of authenticity within the political process so that even processes of listening and consultation come to be seen as questionably honest. Focus groups have attracted some derision and, at the time of writing, complaints are being aired that the public's money is being spent on discovering, but not divulging, its own opinions. Within the political arena the suspicion arises that the outcome of all this may be at best manipulation and at worst deception. The potential effect of this is widespread cynicism – precisely the opposite of the belief that such exercises are attempting to engineer.

The culture of presentation, first developed in the service of commerce, has been vastly reinforced by the extension of its techniques and principles into public organisations. Social services departments have found it necessary to follow suit by developing mission, marketing and impression management through attention to everything from corporate secrecy to corporate socks. The question is: provided the organisation acts with probity and succeeds in meeting its objectives, does any of this matter? I want to argue that in welfare organisations it matters very much and at a rather deeper level than is suggested by the above considerations, important as they are.

In the organisational process that triggered these reflections there was no explicit reference to these issues but there was nevertheless an implied concern with questions of authenticity and trust. Overtly the new supervision policy aimed to transform working relationships between managers and subordinates at all levels in the hierarchy. It was to provide an environment in which the 'real' task could be pursued: the delivery of care in ways which were appropriate to both the nature of care itself (compassionate, sensitive, individuated) and the demands of the institutional environment (efficient, economical).

It was therefore to enable staff to achieve a more productive balance between reflectiveness and effectiveness than had hitherto been possible. The potential tensions were taken for granted as was the fact that operational staff were more likely to emphasise aspects of caring, while the executive was obliged to ensure compliance with the culture of performativity and audit. Hopes that supervision processes would enable these contradictory dimensions of organisational reality to be creatively conjoined were almost universally expressed by managers and social workers alike in various parts of the organisation. However, despite this shared purpose and maturity of response which explicitly drew attention to the need to sustain and work with a contradictory reality, the early months were marked by considerable difficulty.

One of the striking things to emerge in early interviews was the disdain, sometimes verging on contempt, for the supervision folder which was supplied at the launch for the keeping of records. This specially designed folder came complete with corporate logo and compartments containing an array of customised forms for the purposes of record and audit. Considerable thought, and expenditure, had gone into its production and the intended message from the Senior Management Group was that this was a flagship policy of such significance that it justified its own distinctive hardware. However, the cynicism it provoked was captured by one of the interviewees who announced 'the future is laminated'. (In fact it was plastic, but its poetic truth was best captured by 'laminated'.)

The folder had immediately been invested with a set of meanings assigned to it by a resistant and hostile staff group. As the theme reappeared in a number of transcripts, I began to realise that it symbolised a presentation culture concerned with appearance rather than substance, surface rather than depth, performativity rather than authenticity. To some it represented the commodification of human welfare – its expression in fetishistic whimsies. At its most sinister it was an instrument for the evacuation of value, at best a postmodern folly. And yet, 18 months later when the supervision policy had gained widespread acceptance and was, on the whole, working quite well, the project manager announced at a review day that the folders had become rather popular. Regrettably, unused stocks were disappearing – leading to suspicions that staff were 'squirrelling' them away.

What had happened in the interim? How had the significance of this artefact changed so radically? What did this convey of the symbolic world of the organisation: its meanings, myths, metaphors, and mental states? And what light did it shed on the organisational culture? In the first instance, it is important to understand the anxieties that the folder evoked in relation to the major preoccupations of the people who were interviewed. When the transcripts were analysed it became clear that staff were overwhelmingly concerned with improved communication. This emerged as the main locus of their hopes and anxieties. Moreover they explicitly distinguished 'communication' from information systems and instead drew attention to its imaginative, open-ended, sense-making quality and its orientation to understanding. One practitioner said

> *I really would enjoy being part of a larger dialogue – a conversation going on in the department about ways and means.*

There seemed to be a hope that the new policy would facilitate the creation of a dialogic space where formerly there had been a fairly instrumental and politically selective transmission of information. The policy itself had been presented in terms of enhanced accountability in decision-making and better staff development. Communication at either an interpersonal or institutional level had not featured particularly strongly in the discussions which accompanied the launch although it was implied in the notion of a supervision 'chain' linking all levels in the organisation. However, in laying an emphasis on processes which invoked face-to-face interaction, a new aspiration had come into play: the revitalisation of the communicative content of everyday transactions. Analysis of the transcripts revealed many references to problems of meaning and interpretation between managers and managed at all levels in the hierarchy. Persistent refrains such as 'what are management really getting at?' and references to 'game-playing' and 'dodging and weaving' suggested pervasive anxieties over authenticity and sincerity. As if in response to these concerns, meetings with senior managers gave rise to unsolicited assurances of honest intent and at times expressions of grievance that their good faith should seemingly be called into question.

The folders appeared to provide staff with a focus for these worries. They were sometimes described as 'useless' or 'poorly designed' but just as often in the language of consumer contempt: 'tat', 'tacky', 'cheap', and as a waste of precious resources. There seemed to be concern that the leadership, the symbolic 'mind' of the organisation, had in some way lost contact with its 'body' and its energies had been displaced on to a childish diversion. In this regressive 'game' it had lost its way and abandoned any sense of honest realism for inverted values wholly inappropriate to the seriousness of the work that people were doing. How then could such a leadership be trusted?

I would suggest anxiety about the meaning of this small piece of plastic equipment was a highly localised and potent reflection of other more widespread cultural anxieties that were, and still are, affecting social work. These were aroused by the introduction, via the folder, of a commodity aesthetic, experienced as an unwelcome intrusion within a transformational process. The sense in which I use these terms will be clarified in the course of the argument.

At a very general level, writers on post-modern consciousness have for years emphasised the preoccupation of highly consumerised cultures with the appearance of things. The dominant metaphors of visual aesthetics become the iconic image or commercial logo – or else the collage in which any invitation to perceptual depth is sacrificed in favour of a playful disregard of structure, perspective, and tradition. Post-modern aesthetics have provided us with the Disneyesque simulations of the shopping mall and have emancipated public buildings and utilities from functional reference. In London we have intelligence headquarters that would not be out of place in Toytown while the Viennese can revel in a joyous public waste incinerator that recalls the set for a science fiction comedy. This is all very well, but the carnival which is so amusing in architecture has more-ambiguous connotations in welfare organisations.

Howe sums it up substantively and stylistically

Each new encounter simply triggers a fresh set of transactions, negotiations and agreements. It is a here-and-now world; a world without history pattern or direction. Cases do not progress; they are not required to go anywhere in the long run. In a sense it does not matter. It is literally a fiction to explain the present with reference to the past; there is no necessary connection. In the absence of authoritative texts to explain events, sense arises in the immediate 'context' where the client's behaviour, needs and responses meet the social worker's rules resources and procedures. And out of such meetings arise agreements, tasks and time limits. (Howe ,1996 p. 91.)

The abstraction and reductionism implicit in these events (to call them processes would be to presume duration and meaningful sequence) are evidenced by the loss of any requirement to consider the unique psycho-biographical history of the client or even their embodied selves. In the culture of performativity it is behaviours rather than actors that become the focus of attention. Behaviours can be charted, itemised, measured, compared, controlled, and assessed – actors are not so easily characterised. The actor is a complex psycho-social unity and is, first and foremost, a physical presence – a body in all its unremitting finitude with its odours, desires and diseases. While this is in general an all too discomfiting truth, the exuberance of post-modern culture – global travel, cyber-sex, world music, transnational cuisines – represents a defiance of limits for those who can so permit themselves. The welfare candidate is more closely confined.

Zygmunt Bauman's (1999) account of the growing immateriality of the new global order points to one of its most disastrous consequences: the polarisation between the globals and the locals. The lifestyles of the former find an analogue in the movement of finance capital – extraterrestrial and extracorporeal, technologically integrated into the global information order, always on the move, liberated from the confines of territory. The locals on the other hand bear the human costs of this movement of capital, people, and information. They are the 'failed' consumers, more than ever bounded by their bodies and localities.

It seems to me that these same relations are reflected in the way in which some highly managerialised regimes relate to their practitioners and clients. Technical-rational administrations supported by modern information systems illustrate very well the tendency to immateriality when they become enclosed within self-referential and technologically supported loops of assessment, procedure, and audit within which space for the negotiation of meaning in the face-to-face encounters of bodies and brains ('wetware' as it is known to geeks) is systematically reduced. These increasingly instrumental cultures can operate at high levels of immateriality where the rigid and formulaic quality of language and procedure severs them from sensuous connection. Meanwhile practice immerses social workers in impoverished worlds where needs often take on an insistent physical materiality, whether they are to do with comfort levels: the struggle to keep warm or clean or nourished; or the expressive dimensions of life which are inseparable from the body – violence, nurturing, and desire.

What are the psychological counterparts of the growing immateriality of culture? This may be yet another twist to the radical split between body and mind proposed by Descartes and pursued so inventively by western thought and scientific endeavour, including a great deal of contemporary evaluative research. What is the impact on consciousness of this divorce between the mobile and technologically assisted products of human intelligence and the unyielding confinement of the body? The fluctuations of fashion with their ever more invasive manifestations in tattooing and body-piercing, and the normalising of cosmetic surgery as another form of good grooming, fail to alter the fact that bodies are so very disappointing, and so inexorably corruptible. Ageing – always an unforgiving process – is now unforgiven, not least in the world of work. Social work may still be seen as an employment enclave where maturity is valued at the lower echelons, partly because many people embark on it relatively late. However, a very senior manager of a large London department recently observed that in his early fifties he was one of the oldest in his group and would try to 'hang on for a bit' as he had two teenage daughters to educate.

There is good reason to mistrust the body and post-modernist thought with its militant anti-essentialism has made it intellectually respectable to do so. As Adam Phillips (1995) puts it: *the body is misleading because it leads one into relationship and so towards the perils and ecstasies of dependence and risk; it reminds us of the existence of other people* (1995 p. 94).

Phillips's discussion of Winnicott (1964, 1975, 1988) considers the psychological ground of this dualism between body and mind and of the kind of development implied in the sundering of what in the new-born baby appears to be a unity – a 'psyche-soma' in which mind grows out of representations of bodily sensations. It is a response to an environment which is always less than perfectly adapted to the infant's bodily needs and which must therefore be distanced and accounted for in some way in order to be rendered tolerable. Mind develops in the infant as a response to the failures and frustrations of bodies. When it perceives that bodies need and lack, and the maternal body, the source of goodness, is beyond its control, mind allows the infant to hold in fantasy what it cannot have in reality. In good-enough circumstances a healthily developing mind would remain in dynamic tension with the insistent demands and desires of the body allowing for tolerance of pain without denial and both recognition and deferment of pleasure. This is also the basis for the development of trust – an ability to apprehend the durability and reliability of others who are separate. An over-developed mind would be one which attempted to subject all the needs and risks of the body to its regulation. Phillips (1995) points out that from Winnicott's point of view, Descartes's 'I think therefore I am' indicates a failure of development.

Here we have a vital link: the possibility of thinking is intertwined with the discomfiture of physical dependency on a world whose resources we are liable to find meagre in relation to our desires. The overgrowth of mind and denial of the body is a defensive function that gradually extends into cultural life – and nowhere more problematically than within those very institutions which exist to manage the body's vulnerabilities to sickness, poverty, and death. Foucault (1975) insisted that the growth of technologies of regulation within welfare is propelled by the ever-present political imperatives to define, control, categorise, disperse, and exclude the threats to the administrative order represented by physical needs of the poor. Just as the mind, in Phillips's phrase, acts as an 'enraged bureaucrat' attempting to manage the unmanageable emotional impositions that constantly return us to the body, administration acts as its external socially structured counterpart – managing the disruptive chaotic claims that arise from the all-too-materially-needy lives of clients. The language and methods of needs and risk assessment and classification, and the evaluative technologies that measure outcomes serve, among other things, to translate these thick and complex needs into abstract measurable entities which can be set against a series of procedurally defined norms.

Commodity aesthetics are an aspect of cultural immateriality. The commodity, Marx tells us, is 'a very queer thing' that, despite its trivial appearance, 'abounds in metaphysical subtleties and theological niceties' (Marx, 1965 p. 71). The mystical nature of the commodity form depends on its abstraction from the sensuous: from the labour that produced it and the human relations that it conceals. Once produced as a commodity the value of an object has no connection with its unique physical properties. Warhol's Marilyn Monro is as endlessly reproducible as his cans of tomato soup. However, the question of why commodity aesthetics may be incongruent with the culture of an organisation whose purpose is the delivery of social care needs to be examined a little further. In the organisation in question the folder was explicitly seen by staff as symptomatic of the commodification of care and was therefore directly linked to wider cultural discourses. Although dislike of it was widespread, only 3 out of 40 people voiced direct political criticisms. I want to suggest that while it was offered as a means of capturing transformational aspirations, the contradiction between the promise of a commodity aesthetic and a transformational object (Bollas, 1987) that people could use creatively was simply too great.

The idea of the transformational object was developed by Christopher Bollas (1987) in his consideration of the nature of the aesthetic moment and its relationship to early experiences of care. Bollas considers the psychodynamics of aesthetic recognition, and asks where the experience comes from. Why is it that faced with a symphony, song, or story, or a picture, building, or garden, we sometimes get that uncanny emotional/physical sensation that moves or disturbs us. Bollas suggests that this is not so much due to a projection of desire, as a use of the aesthetic object as container of the wish for transformation. This becomes possible because of the way in which it becomes a vector for a form of recollection. It allows us to re-enact the quality of the early experience of transformation in the presence of the first transformational object – the facilitating mother.

The primary aesthetic then is irrevocably linked to the experience of care – the mother's particular way of being with her baby and providing an environment which modifies sensations of pleasure and discomfiture. The manner of her care – her particular way of feeding, holding, cooing, stroking – is internalised and patterns what Bollas calls a personalised 'aesthetic of being' which will affect all future ways of handling the self and being with others. For the most part I was not raised by my own mother, who was figuratively and literally in 'another country' for most of my childhood. My relations with her were distant and often difficult, yet when my son was born after a complicated labour my spontaneous words to him reached back across more than a quarter of a century to a long-forgotten phrase of hers from my infancy – 'What a pickle!' In the months that followed I caught myself again and again (and by no means always with pleasurable nostalgia) re-enacting in barely definable ways her personal idiom of care and years later I see its imprint still in my daughter's care of her pets – in her voice and gestures, and her affectionate humorous bossiness.

Bollas argues that the intensity of the aesthetic experience that arises in adult life evokes an uncanny sense of fusion and possibility which accompanied our earliest experiences of transformation. Advertising implicitly recognises this, playing strongly on the hopes we invest in a holiday, a new outfit, a change of car, or a perfume. Although these commodities hold out a promise of future change, the particular things that 'hook' us do so because they recall a past accomplishment:

> *never cognitively apprehended but existentially known. . . . This anticipation of being transformed by an object . . . inspires the subject with a reverential attitude towards it, so that even though the transformation of the self will not take place on the scale it reached during early life, the adult subject tends to nominate such objects as sacred* (Bollas, 1987 p.17).

If our capacity to invest aesthetically in objects depends on a sense of transformational promise which has something of the sacred about it, it is likely that non-investment or disinvestment invokes a sense of the profane – and profanity leads to particularly virulent denigration. It may be that the key to the difference between what we choose to identify as 'art' and commodity aesthetics lies in the fact that commodities, by their very nature, hold our investment fleetingly and precariously. When we reject them we despise them – their promise is revealed as a sham. Last year my (young adult) children fought in the attic for possession of a plastic sportsbag once rejected as contemptibly 'sad', now redesignated 'Adidas-retro'. The rapid illusionment and disillusionment with objects of consumption are trivial enough where sportsbags are concerned, but an aesthetic of care requires a more durable and reliable transformational object. It demands the kind of responsiveness that can only be evoked by the presence of another who withstands our denigration because in their personal idiom of care they hail us as subjects, rather than consumers, and in turn demand our recognition. This comes closer to describing the claim of art than the claim of the commodity. The rejection of the supervision folders arose because in their plastic ephemerality they evoked a commodity aesthetic at the very moment when hopes for relational transformation in the presence of another were at their height.

There is a joke (post-modern or Marxist – depending how you read it) which declares that the unhappiest of men is the fetishist who longs for a shoe and has to make do with the whole woman. This captures something of Marx's concept of commodity fetishism which at its simplest identifies 'a definite social relation between men, that assumes, in their eyes, the fantastic form of a relation between things' (Marx, 1965 p. 72). Hinschelwood (1985, 1989) suggests that the psychological correlative of this alienation is that bits of identity and human relations are projected onto things where they appear as the property, not of people, but of those things themselves. The thing-like character of these human attributes then obscures their mutable origins in emotions and relationships and acquires fixity and resistance to change. Their ideological function is then to promote a mentality of 'no alternatives' whereby, for example, the commodification of care takes on the character of a natural order and all scepticism is denigrated as loss of contact with reality. The important point, as Zizec (1989) makes clear, is not merely that things replace people – although in social care we should at least be vigilant about this – but that there is a fundamental misrecognition at work, an abstraction whereby a part comes to be an equivalent of the whole. This property of equivalence then inheres in the part as one of its essential characteristics. The supreme commodity form is of course money, but could be shoes. It is not merely that a particular woman is symbolically desired through her shoe (she would still then be a mediated object of desire). Rather, the shoe takes on the equivalent properties of a desirable woman which it retains quite apart from its relation to its owner. The eroticisation of the shoe depends on these abstracted qualities while the wearer becomes dispensable, or worse, a positive hindrance to the realisation of desire.

The alienation of the fetishist lies not in his choice of symbols but in the way in which the symbol becomes a symptom (Zizec, 1989), a pathological manifestation of human relations which appears to have a logic and life of its own at the expense of the health of its hosts. This suggests another reason why the commodity form makes for a very poor transformational object. The point about the good-enough facilitating mother/environment is that she has a life of her own but does not assert it at the expense of the infant whose receptivity to her idiom of care depends on a non-intrusive attentiveness in the context of a sensual, loving, and immediately personal presence. In later life it is the symbol, not the symptom, of this connection that evokes possibilities of change.

The implications of this for social welfare are far from trivial. In the first instance it suggests that we should be concerned at the intrusion of commodity aesthetics and the culture of presentationalism that introduces them because they are at odds with the nature of care and are likely to obscure or distort our apprehension of its emotional and relational content. The case of the folders illustrated this and more. I mentioned earlier that after a year or so they no longer invited contempt and were reportedly becoming popular. I doubt that this was because they had finally been invested with the properties of a transformational object. It is more likely that as the immediate face-to-face relationships were revitalised through what, in effect, was a rather good policy, the experience of substantive transformation displaced any symptomatic function and the folder was appreciated for its use-value. However, there was evidence in the transcripts of later interviews of a more interesting factor at work: the emergence of a narrative or biographical aesthetic altogether more appropriate to human caring. It seemed that as people established the relational context, or in Winnicott's terms the 'transitional space' of supervision, communicative processes were regenerated and this was reflected in the telling of stories – about organisational mythologies and their debunking, about the hopes and failures of change, above all about human idiosyncrasy and the particular contributions of individuals. There was a notable turning outwards from a preoccupation with internal dynamics of the organisation to the work with clients, and these stories were richly embellished with example.

Social work has had a historical affinity for narrative and there is insufficient space here to develop an account of its problems and possibilities. (See Froggett, 2000 forthcoming.) From the perspective of this paper it is their transformational potential and their relationship to supervision which are most important. Good supervision operates very much as a transitional space analogous to the neutral arena presided over by the facilitative mother. Within it the emotional containment and suspension of instrumental demands allow the child to undertake a creative and playful reality-testing. These experimental endeavours – transitional phenomena, as Winnicott called them – revolve around the distinction between 'in here' and 'out there' and are basically the ground from which thought and cultural life develop. As Day Sclator (1997) has argued, stories are transitional phenomena in that they allow for exploration of reality through the playful linking of inner and outer worlds, the personal and the social. This is why the narrative is such a seemingly natural, enjoyable, and accessible way of conveying the mutability of experience and why it allows us to 'dabble in the subjunctive' (Bruner, 1990). This is the imaginative 'as if' that fosters an elasticity of thought whereby we can both recognise reality and reconfigure, events, emotions, and concepts in an effort to reinvent the future. It allows people to deal paradox, to find new solutions and even to negotiate between ideal and reality, for example between reflectiveness and effectiveness.

A narrative aesthetic is ill-suited to the fetishist, firstly in that it inclines towards complexity through the linking of very different domains which otherwise tend to be kept separate. It impels us to apprehend parts in terms of the changing networks of relations that constitute a whole. It often does this through humour or parable connecting seemingly disparate areas of experience such as states of minds, organisational relationships, and political discourses. Secondly, by locating events in real time it reintroduces a sense of history, movement, and process where a commodity aesthetic – of things which are here or gone, like the passing of fashions – suggests an eternal present. It is therefore well adapted to the understanding and recounting of change. Finally, it lends itself to recognition, tolerance, and inclusiveness. It is an intrinsically interpersonal form in which the story-teller cannot help but draw attention to his or her own standpoint, and at the same draw in other voices.

From the point of view of policy implementation one of the most important points to arise from all this is that powerful discourses can position the unwitting subject in ways which may not suit their purposes and can have unintended practical effects. Performativity and presentationalism encouraged staff to respond to a rather banal object in terms of its commodity aesthetics rather than its utility. It took on for a while an unanticipated and unhelpful importance, quite independently of anyone's intentions. This dissipated as an aesthetic adequate to the materiality of care was discovered in the context of communicative relationships.

Perhaps I shall be seen as making a lot out of a little. If so, consider Marx's delightful description of a table which

> *continues to be that common, everyday thing, wood. But so soon as it steps forth as a commodity, it is changed into something transcendent. It not only stands with its feet on the ground, but, in relation to all other commodities, it stands on its head, and evolves out of its wooden brain grotesque ideas, far more wonderful than 'table-turning' ever was.* (Marx, 1965 p. 71.)

Notes
1. With many thanks to my neighbour the late Robert Hopper who planted this idea one day over the garden wall.

References

Bauman, Z (1999) *Globalisation* Oxford, Blackwell/Polity Press

Bollas, C (1987) *The Shadow of the Object* London, Free Association Books

Bruner, J (1990) *Acts of Meaning* Cambridge, Harvard University Press

Day Sclater, S (1997) Creating the Self: stories as transitional phenomena. *Paper presented at Auto/biography Study Group Annual Conference. Methodology Matters* University of Cambridge

Descartes, R (1986) *Meditations on First Philosophy* (trans. John Cottingham) Cambridge, Cambridge University Press

Foucault (1979) *Discipline and Punish* Harmondsworth, Peregrine Books

Froggett, L (1999a) Sustaining Tensions in Practice Supervision. *Social Services Research 1* 1999 pp 33-42

Froggett, L (1999b) Staff Supervision and Dependency Culture: a case study. *Social Work and Social Sciences Review* (forthcoming)

Froggett, L (2000) *Love, Hate and Welfare* Birmingham, Venture Press (forthcoming)

Hinschelwood, R D (1985) Projective Identification, Alienation and Society. *Group Analysis* 18, 3 pp 241-54

Hinschelwood, R D (1989) Social Possession of Identity in (ed.) Richards, B, *The Crises of the Self* London, Free Association Books

Howe, D (1996) *Surface and Depth in Social Work Practice* London, Routledge

Marx, K (1965) *Capital Vol. 1* London. Lawrence and Wishart

Phillips, A (1995) *Terrors and Experts* London. Faber & Faber

Winnicott, D W (1964) *The Child the Family and the Outside World* London, Penguin

Winnicott, D W (1975) *Through Paediatrics to Psychoanalysis* London, Hogarth Press

Winnicott, D W (1988) *Human Nature* London, Free Association Books

Zizec, S (1989) *The Sublime Object of Ideology* London, Verso

Chapter 3
Defining Good Social Work: aspects of social control
Julian Buchanan and Malcolm Millar

Introduction

The social work profession needs to become much clearer about its actual and potential identity. We shall defend this view by focusing largely on the controlling functions of social work, arguing the need to incorporate into practice an explicit preparedness to take decisions aimed at controlling the behaviour of people. Control, we shall suggest, is a legitimate aim which, properly pursued, need not induce a sense of guilt or embarrassment in those who aim to develop good practice. One major reason for considering it necessary to clarify the significance of control in social work is that in recent years it has become unfashionable to discuss this aspect of practice. As will be noted below, the values of empowerment and anti-oppression have come to the fore, and these values have at times seemed hard to square with practice which can centrally involve the restriction of liberty. We shall argue that reference to such values, while potentially beneficial to social work, can also be misleading for those who seek to define good practice.

We must acknowledge at the outset that an emphasis upon the legitimacy of controlling aspects of social work practice might seem a little odd, given the recent history of the profession. Over the past 20 years social work commentators have consistently expressed unease at the increasing use of controlling measures, particularly in state social work. Jordan noted the problems caused by a diminishing supply of resources available for helping people, and has associated these with a more prominent monitoring and surveillance function for social workers (Jordan, 1988). Social workers seem to have less and less to offer, apart from a watchful and potentially alienating presence. Jones and Novak warn that political decisions of recent years have led to the increasing regulation of social work, and that this has served to divert practice away from any real helping function and towards the identification and control of those who are most dangerous (Jones and Novak, 1993). This point is borne out, specifically in the field of child protection, by three major studies that emerged in Britain during the 1990s. They identified a preoccupation with the management of risk to children which drew too many families into the net of 'child protection', with insufficient developmentof more-informal frameworks of social work help (Cleaver and Freeman, 1995; Farmer and Owen, 1995).

In the context of these, not unrepresentative, observations is it not vital to challenge the drift towards control which has gained momentum in recent times? Surely, it may be argued, there is a need to contest those measures which have turned social workers into functionaries of a state that does not care, and which so often excludes and marginalises vulnerable people.

We have no wish to add to the miseries of the masses of people who have multiple needs, and who may experience the interventions of the social worker as insensitive, intrusive, and unhelpful. We shall, however, defend the view that the absence of clear thinking about the controlling aspects of social work has been a major barrier to the development of a coherent account of what good social work should involve. We shall also argue that this lack of clarity has had detrimental effects on the communication between workers and clients, and that this is partly responsible for difficulties in worker:client relations. First, it is necessary to take a closer look at what has been happening to social work in recent years.

Pressures for change
These are difficult if not critical times for social work in Britain. Several processes have combined to influence and restructure the work of practitioners. We shall not rehearse these in great detail here, but a summary of some of the key elements is necessary.

First, the past 20 years have seen a proliferation of legislative frameworks, policies, and procedures. 'Managerialism' has become a dominant feature of social work provision so that practice has shifted from the use of discretionary professional judgements in ongoing work with clients towards intensively prescribed and monitored interventions. This top-down approach has been encouraged and sustained not only by the drive for economic efficiency but also by the cumulative fall-out from several heavily publicised inquiries over the past 25 years – particularly into social work with child abuse. (See Saraga, 1993 for an overview.)

Second, the prescriptivist and managerialist tendency has increasingly figured in the education and training of social workers. In the 1990s the Central Council for the Education and Training of Social Work (CCETSW) overhauled the social workers' qualification the Certificate of Qualification in Social Work, and introduced the 'competence based' Diploma in Social Work which was itself subject to further revision. Through the development of 'partnerships' between social work agency employers and teaching institutions, the new DipSW was constructed to provide a preparation for practice which was supposedly improved by being more in tune with the day-to-day tasks which practitioners undertook. One major consequence was the reining in of the autonomy of the academic institutions and an increase in the influence of social work agencies. The value of this move has been strongly disputed (Webb, 1996; Jones, 1996). What is undeniable is that it presupposed that social work was an activity that *required* redefinition, and that it was necessary to regulate training along the 'competence based' lines which the new definition entailed. There was, as Webb has noted with regard to social work education, a perceived 'failure to deliver reliability of product' (Webb, 1996, p.177).

Third, as social workers in the statutory sector have become more involved in managing budgets, and in developing and purchasing 'packages' of care which they do not themselves implement, their traditional role as professional helpers of persons in difficulty has diminished. The caring part of social work has increasingly been seen as one than can be 'contracted out' to relatively unskilled personnel (Cochrane, 1993). This 'purchaser:provider' split in the delivery of social services has raised the question whether statutory social workers will in the future continue to practise social work in the traditional sense of the term which incorporates the provision of care. Will they have a helping role, as distinct from one which centres round a form of 'assessment' that confines itself to narrowly defined criteria for judging immediate risk, balancing this alongside diminishing and competing budgetary demands?

Besieged social workers?
The events and developments briefly recounted above have been crucial in shaping the way in which social workers are trained and in determining the nature of their tasks. It is not surprising, therefore, that some within social work have questioned their own role, and have asked whether their daily encounters with some of the most desperate and vulnerable people in society should be handled in the functional and often cursory manner that agency policies have increasingly seemed to necessitate.The concern with 'competence' insisted upon by CCETSW, while superficially useful in so far as it can seem to offer an alternative to 'incompetent' practice, has contributed little to the social worker's clarity of purpose. It has not touched upon the feelings of personal and professional inadequacy, which are almost inevitably experienced when working in the face of multiple deprivation. The extent of the demand for services caused by the increasing poverty of years of 'welfare restructuring' has, as John Clarke has noted, 'consequences for social work in the form of

client bombardment' (Clarke, 1996, p 50). Listing a set of 'competences' skates over this issue. It does not address the question raised by so much social work: how can practice *ever* be competent, given the nature and scale of the problems confronted?

Articulation of a vision

So, we live in times when many in social work have become exhausted by a succession of changes which they would reject or at least call into question, and when they are forced to confront deprivations and disadvantages which they are ill-equipped to ameliorate. From one point of view, it might be thought remarkable that a highly ambitious vision of good practice has developed which focuses precisely upon those processes of oppression, social exclusion, and disempowerment which can make day-to-day practice seem so inadequate and ineffectual.

However, as we know, ideas of opposition to oppression and of empowering social work clients have proved very influential indeed in social work. They have dominated much of the recent literature in the field, and have featured prominently amongst key texts for social work practice (see, for example, Dominelli,1988; Langan and Day, 1992; Thompson, 1993). Part of the reason for this is that social work has *always* maintained a concern for the particular experience and point of view of those people in society whom we have recently learnt to call 'excluded'. One of the things which is more distinctive of recent times is that there has been an accumulation of evidence suggesting that inequality and social exclusion are on the increase, making it seem perfectly logical that these things must be opposed with renewed vigour. Furthermore, the values associated with this opposition to oppressive and discriminatory trends have seemed to offer a positive, and much needed, way of describing what the profession fundamentally stands for. It is understandable that social work, buffeted by the vicissitudes of recent years, has been drawn towards assertions such as Thompson's 'good practice is anti-discriminatory practice' (Thompson, 1993, p.10).

We are not contesting the thesis that an understanding of oppression, discrimination, and inequality should be an essential part of a social worker's conceptual framework. Embracing the 'bigger picture' of oppression and its individual consequences highlights the need for practitioners and social work agencies to be self-critical in their decision-making and to be alive to the power-differentials pervading the experences and life-chances of social work clients. Equipped with this critical approach, social work 'assessment' is less likely to slide into the kind of diagnostic mode which reduces personal difficulties to personal deficiencies. Instead, there is recognition that many clients' 'needs' are a product of pathologising thought-systems and/or policy frameworks. Problems such as child abuse (Parton, 1985), crime (Jordan, 1988), women's mental health (Ussher, 1992), and domestic violence (Dobash and Dobash,1992) have all been analysed ways that bring out their distinctively social dimension – and these analyses are extremely valuable in social work practice.

Accepting all of this, our key concern is with the practical significance of those ideas, such as anti-oppression, empowerment and so on, which have just been referred to. Do they lead us towards good practice in the rather straightforward way which often seems to be suggested? We think not. The concepts in question have rarely been subjected to the kind of close scrutiny which would have tested their robustness in the face of many of the tasks social workers have to carry out.

Social work, empowerment, and control

An essential component of social work should involve the promotion of the rights and opportunities of the individual, and this entails recognition of the powerful structural factors that impinge upon those rights and opportunities. The importance and relevance of this core function are clearly grasped when considering, for example, social work involvement with a black school-child who is truanting and under-achieving in a predominantly white school. Alternatively, consider the position of a woman subject to violence and abuse from her male partner. Examples such as these can be developed to illustrate the need to move away from pathologising analysis towards a broader politicised vision of social work that incorporates an understanding of the impact of structural discrimination and oppression. Each of these cases involves inequalities in the distribution of power, and we might say that a social worker's role would consist at least partly in an attempt to help liberate those who are suffering the effects of inequality.

However, consider the role of a social worker working with a lone mother with two pre-school children, who injects a gramme of street heroin a day and pays for the habit through burglary and shoplifting. Her children are on the child protection register as a consequence of serious bruising for which the mother is thought to be responsible (though she denies this). Can social work in this case accurately be described in terms of the transfer of power to the parent? Not staightforwardly. It may well be argued that there are disempowering forces in society which would be acting upon a woman in this situation. But the woman is herself infringing the rights of others who are the victims of her offending. She may also be placing her children at risk.

In cases such as this, social work intervention may involve control – it may entail the restriction of liberty. The woman mentioned above is probably subject to oppression and discrimination, but it does not follow from this that she has freedom to make choices which place others at risk. Nor does it follow from the fact that social workers are operating in a British society which is, arguably, to a significant degree more unequal and divisive than it was 20 years ago that they should somehow compensate for this by not intervening in a way that restricts choice to some degree. Social work clients have rights, but they do not have rights which legitimate harming other people. And, crucially, the social worker – by becoming a social worker – assumes a role which is partly concerned with furthering the interests and rights of those in society who may suffer from the actions of the people who are formally recognised as 'clients' or 'service users'.

Some of the points just made may appear to have a commonplace quality, particularly to people involved in the realities of practice. But it is important to ask where the values of anti-oppression and empowerment stand in relation to these 'commonplaces'. In fact, such values have sometimes been appealed to in ways implying that restrictive and controlling interventions are dubious or dysfunctional *per se*, and are therefore incapable of being classified within the parameters of good practice.

This view, we should argue, is seriously mistaken. What is needed is a shift in thinking at the level of the theory and the values which have *seemed* to offer a useful and secure vision of social work in recent years. Recourse to the controlling functions of social work would not therefore be seen *in itself* as providing evidence that practice had failed or fallen short. Nor would practitioners – conscious of the ideals of empowerment – pursue control guiltily, or with that peculiar furtiveness that comes from the failure to be transparent about one's concerns. The need for social control is thus accepted as a given, and once this way of thinking is established it becomes easier to see the need for a more detailed exploration of the criteria which socially controlling practice must satisfy. Explicitness about the value of, and need for, social control is a precondition for clarity about the circumstances and the manner in which controlling measures should be taken.

By way of illustration, it is worth drawing attention to one example of how, in the absence of openness about controlling functions, a supposedly empowering approach has been argued to have detrimental effects. Some research on the participation of parents at child protection conferences has shown how procedures aimed at involving parents in these conferences, although portrayed as empowering, can be seriously deceptive (Corby, Millar and Young, 1996; Corby and Millar, 1997). Although parents attending child protection conferences were generally glad they had done so in order to see what was being said, they also tended to feel alienated and mistrustful of the decision-making process. Ideas of partnership and empowerment were not borne out by the experienced reality. The researchers found that parents felt unable to disagree with professionals, or to negotiate a way forward which seriously took into account their own perspectives on child care. Ultimately, parents were unclear about what was expected of them because this issue was not tackled with sufficient clarity. They felt, in a sense, 'disempowered' by the purportedly empowering procedures. The failure of the social workers to deal directly with the issues of control (concerns about child abuse) left the parents uncertain and confused.

The point of introducing this illustration is not to maintain that social work with families in child protection work should avoid a concern for strategies aimed at helping parents and their children. It is that this type of work inevitably generates situations which place the issue of control on the agenda, and that it is easy to deal with this in a way that submerges the controlling aspect of the work in a rhetoric of empowerment, partnership, and so on. To re-emphasise the point made earlier, it is vital to accept that social work intervention can be, and should sometimes be, socially controlling. Once this is accepted, questions must then be raised about when controlling measures should be taken, how they should be taken, and when they cease to become necessary. Unless these questions are thoroughly explored, the basis upon which practitioners take decisions will be unclear, both to the practitioners themselves and to the 'clients' they encounter.

Learning from probation?
As a concluding thought, we should like to refer with approval to an aspect of probation practice which exemplifies the openness about social control which we think is necessary. The offence focus in probation practice has been developed over the past 15 years. It crucially involves the assumption that probation is fundamentally about tackling reoffending. This is made clear to people subject to probation supervision, and it is clear to probation services and their employees who know that they are supposed to develop effective ways of carrying out their main business.

Now there are many who would say that Probation has gone too far along a 'correctionalist' path, paying insufficient attention to the factors of structural oppression and social disadvantage which contextualise much offending behaviour. Indeed, we are on record as expressing concerns about both this, and also about the fact that agency policies built around the offence focus which risk losing that peculiar responsiveness to individuality which has traditionally been viewed a feature of good social work (Buchanan and Millar, 1997). However, the *principle* of the offence focus is to be welcomed inasmuch as it incorporates those characteristics of explicitness about control which social work practice in other areas has sometimes lacked. Furthermore, being clear about the principal aim of working to enable the avoidance of further offending provides the basis for asking how this is best achieved, i.e. through the development of a relevant knowledge and theory base concerning offending and offenders. This process can and should include attempts to help and encourage the use of greater self-control on the part of offenders, and it should also involve practical help aimed at reducing those social or economic pressures which can make offending seem a good course of action.

Could a branch of social work like child protection practice benefit from a similar approach? There are, we should suggest, clear parallels to be drawn. Practitioners need a knowledge and theory base which is centred on the phenomenon of child abuse. The socially controlling steps which practioners take should be informed by this knowledge, and workers should be able to explain why they are doing what they are doing. The decisions taken may involve restrictions of freedom, but they should have an authority which does not merely come from the social worker's power but from a rationale for intervention which can be made explicit.

What is being outlined here may, in fact, be described as a kind of empowering practice. For, paradoxically, in accepting that interventions are often at odds with 'client's' own perceived interests and needs, it points to the need for justification of these interventions – the client has a right to know why his or her liberty is restricted and a right not to be soft-talked into acceptance of this kind of restriction without the genuine option of argument or negotiation. This is a kind of empowerment but, crucially, it is rooted deep in the reality of the complex and often conflictual activity which probation practice, and much social work practice, entails.

References
Buchanan, J and Millar, M (1997) 'Probation: Reclaiming a Social Work Identity' *Probation Journal* 44, pp 32-6

Clarke, J (1996) 'After Social Work?' in Parton, N (ed.) *Social Theory, Social Change and Social Work* London, Routledge, pp 36-60

Cleaver, H and Freeman, P (1995) *Parental Perspectives in Cases of Suspected Child Abuse* London, HMSO

Cochrane, A (1993) 'Challenges from the Centre' in Clarke, J (ed.) *A Crisis in Care?* Milton Keynes, OUP pp 69-101

Corby, B and Millar, M (1997) 'A Parents' View of Partnership' in Bates, J, Pugh, R and Thompson, N (eds) *Protecting Children: Challenges and Change* Aldershot, Arena pp??

Corby, B, Millar, M and Young, L (1996) 'Parental Participation in Child Protection Work: Rethinking the Rhetoric' *British Journal of Social Work* 26. pp 475-492

Dobash, R E and Dobash, R P (1992) *Women, Violence and Social Change* London, Routledge

Dominelli, L (1988) *Anti-Racist Social Work* Basingstoke, Hants and London, Macmillan

Farmer, E and Owen, M (1995) *Child Protection Practice: Public Risks and Private Remedies* London, HMSO

Jones, C (1996) 'Anti-intellectualism and the peculiarities of British social work education', in Parton, N (ed.) *Social Theory, Social Change and Social Work* London, Routledge pp 190-210

Jones, C and Novak, T (1993) 'Social Work Today' in *British Journal of Social Work* 23. pp 195-212

Jordan, B (1988) 'Poverty, Social Work and the State' in Becker, S and MacPherson, S (eds) *Public Issues, Private Pain* London, Insight, pp 340-349

Langan, M and Day, L (1992) *Women, Oppression and Social Work* London, Routledge

Parton, N. (1985) T*he Politics of Child Abuse* London, Macmillan

Saraga, E (1993) 'The Abuse of Children' in Dallos, R and McLaughlin, E (eds) *Social Problems and the Family* London, Sage

Thompson, N (1993) *Anti-Discriminatory Practice* (Second Edition), London, BASW

Ussher, J (1992) 'Science Sexing Psychology: Positivistic Science and Gender Bias in Clinical Psychology', in Ussher, J and Nicholson, P (eds) *Gender Issues in Clinical Psychology* London, Routledge, pp 39-67

Webb, D (1996) 'Regulation for the Radicals; the State, CCETSW and the Academy', in Parton, N, (ed.) *Social Theory, Social Change and Social Work* London, Routledge, pp 172-189

Chapter 4
Taking Oppression Seriously: A critique of managerialism in social work/probation
Mike Nellis

Introduction

'People always get what they ask for; the only trouble is that they never know, until they get it, what it actually is that they have asked for.'
Aldous Huxley.

This chapter seeks to query the way in which the anti-oppressive paradigm has been developed in the literature on social work values, and in the practice of social workers and probation officers. It asks why the idea of oppression has been applied, often appropriately, if a little indiscriminately and in a strangely exclusive way, only to issues of race, gender, age, disability and sexuality, and not to the managerialist practices with which social work and probation are now so thoroughly infused. Managerialism as a practice and an ideology is sufficiently corrosive of personal autonomy to qualify as a form of oppression in its own right, but there is within the social work and probation worlds (henceforth, for brevity, 'social work/probation') 'a deliberation deficit' in respect of this, for which the university departments that train social workers and probation officers bear a significant, but by no means lone, responsibility.

The concept of 'a deliberation deficit' comes from Jeffrey C Goldfarb's (1998) thesis in 'Civility and Subversion: the intellectual in democratic society'. Goldfarb argues that intellectuals, broadly defined, play crucial roles 'in the ongoing practices of democratic life' and that without them 'democratic performance ends in failure'. He believes that the diversity, complexity and pace of change in contemporary western democracies require detailed deliberation if politically viable and ethically defensible ways forward are to be found. For him, it is the task of intellectuals, from a variety of standpoints, to subvert common-sense orthodoxies and sustain civilised deliberation on issues of public concern. I want to apply this argument on a smaller scale, to recent developments in social work/probation, but with the full democratic dimension remaining in the background.

My account must necessarily begin with a glance at the rise of anti-oppressive values in social work, for two reasons. Firstly it is from these values that social work has acquired a self-conception and a public reputation for being concerned with oppression, in particular racism, sexism, etc. Secondly, there has been from their inception, persistent claims that these values were flawed, simplistic, and insufficiently theorised, an authoritarian narrow-minded orthodoxy which was being imposed on staff and students, and thence inscribed in the policies of social work agencies. This critique sees the paradigm dismissed by the heavily ironic and analytically unhelpful term 'political correctness', and then complicated by the occasional willingness of those so accused to appropriate the term as a badge of honour. For present purposes, the idea that merely opening up discourse on race, gender, and sexuality – a clear instance of intellectual subversion in Golfarb's terms – is authoritarian need not detain us. It is the view of Right-wing commentators discomfited by the prospect of discussing these issues on anyone's terms but their own, and who used social work's preoccupation with them as a way to discredit the profession as a whole (Douglas, 1999).

But, issues of content aside, the claim that the anti-oppressive paradigm has been promoted in an authoritarian way warrants enquiry, for that criticism is not the preserve of the Right alone (see Marsh and Triseliotis, 1997 for some evidence of this on DipSWs). Insufficient attention has been paid, in social work/probation to the fact that, as far back as 1994, no less a black intellectual than Stuart Hall, a man with imperishably Left credentials, noted the 'confrontational, in-your-face mode of address' of the paradigm, admitted wryly that 'a strong strain of moral self righteousness has often been [its] most characteristic voice', conceded that some 'undeniable idiocies [had been] committed in the name of anti-racism, anti-sexism and anti-homophobia' and concluded that it was a vanguardist tactic 'with no proper understanding of the centrality of an "educative" conception of politics and the winning of consent to the effective pursuit of the "culture wars"' (Hall, 1994:168-178). In terms very similar to Goldfarb he made the case for robust civil exchange as the essence of politics in a pluralist society:

> *Unless it [ie the anti-oppressive paradigm] is coupled with a strategy which is democratic – in the sense that it genuinely addresses the real fears, confusions, the anxieties as well as the pleasures of ordinary people, tries to educate them to new conceptions of life, to win them over and thus to constitute majorities where there are now only frag-mented minorities – it is destined to fail in the long run, whatever its little local successes*
> (idem:177).

Social work values: memory and forgetting

There are numerable accounts of the ways in which conceptions of social work values have changed over the past 20 years (Hugman and Smith, 1995; Briskman and Noble, 1999). They mostly identify a shift from the ostensibly Kantian [liberal] tradition of respecting persons, and focused on the welfare of individuals, towards more politicised values (characterised as anti-discrimination and anti-oppressiveness). These latter values recognise [some of] the structural inequalities and cultural biases that shape the lives and identities of individuals, and seek to challenge them, not just to provide welfare or care. The focus of anti-oppressive social work has largely been been on identity politics – racism, sexism, ageism, disablism and heterosexism. Sometimes, it has included anti-poverty strategies, and sometimes it has touched on class. At its heart has been a concern with inequality, marginalisation, and exclusion. The goal of social work has been less to care for and help people and more to empower individuals as members – or, more accurately, as exemplars – of these excluded groups.

There is an understandable tendency in contemporary texts on social work values to portray so-called liberal values as inadequate to challenging oppression, particularly in respect of gender and race. There is truth in this, in so far as certain formulations of liberal social work values were focused narrowly on the minutiae of the professional:client relationship, and were also, as Pearson (1975) showed, easily deformed by bureaucratic requirements. But this critique fails to disentangle from liberalism in general a strand of thought which significantly affected the development of social work (and probation) in the post-war period, as well as the lives of some social workers themselves. This was the impact (mostly via America) of the humanistic psychiatrists and psychotherapists – Victor Frankl, Eugene Heimler, Bruno Bettleheim, and Erich Fromm were the key ones – whose work, in some but not all instances triggered by personal experience of concentration camps, developed as a reaction to totalitarianism. Above and beyond the development of techniques for healing damaged individuals, they were concerned to understand the social and psychological roots of extreme authoritarianism, and to contribute to a climate in which it could never flourish again. After the war they added into their concerns the dehumanising effects of mass society as they perceived it in the west – the creation of a docile, 'organisation man' – and warned against what Bettleheim (1960:75) called 'the danger to autonomy in our society'.

Erich Fromm is the only one of the above names that Younghusband (1978:85) mentions as getting 'into the bloodstream of British social work', and there is a chapter of social work history yet to be written about the impact of anti-fascist sentiments – and the intense humanism to which they gave rise – on psychotherapy, counselling, and social work. The near-reverence for the depth and complexity of individual human beings, and the premium which is attached to self-determination and non-directiveness, which characterise humanistic psychology was in part a reaction to the depersonalising and coercive features of totalitarianism. Sadly, those associated with that post-war movement tend already to have been forgotten by social work educators in the 1990s, and by dint of being associated with discredited approaches (those deriving from psychoanalysis) the values that were entwined with them have easily been dismissed as lightweight and anachronistic. None the less, it remains at best odd, and at worst suspicious, that the contemporary protagonists of anti-oppressiveness should have shown no interest in, and sensed no affinity with, the social work thinking that emerged from 'the psychoanalytic *émigré's* uncompromising rejection of Nazism' (Stuart-Hughes, 1975:195).

Conceptions of oppression
There are, not surprisingly, significant differences in the two groups' respective conceptions of oppression. The humanist psychotherapists, writing before the advent of second wave feminism and the American civil rights movement, were not primarily concerned with equality and the empowerment of excluded minorities, although the legacy of anti-semitism ensured some attention to them. They were more concerned with the development of the self and the achievement of full human potential, with the psychology of what Fromm called the 'fear of freedom' (which may make authoritarianism seem appealing), and with understanding the roots of cruelty and destructive behaviour. Alongside the political theorists who were part of the same broadly humanist movement they were staunch promoters of democratic organisational forms, ever vigilant for signs of incipient authoritarianism and abuses of power. They conceived of oppression largely as something which compelled people, whether through coercion or engineered consent, to become mere functionaries in organisations, depriving them of autonomy and the possibility of self-realisation, subjecting them endlessly to rules, orders and propaganda. In the work of Eric Fromm, for example, concern with the psychic and the political was seamlessly interwoven.

Although there are points of connection, contemporary forms of anti-oppressive theory have a rather different focus. They have largely been concerned with identity politics in an imperfect democracy, with gaining space for the identities of people excluded from mainstream institutions and mainstream culture – primarily women, black people, disabled people, old people, gay people. Anti-oppressive practice has involved giving voice to the concerns of marginalised people, 'empowering' them, securing equal opportunities for them, and challenging the attitudes of dominant groups who resist this. It encompasses critiques of the state, ideology, legislation, policy, culture as well as challenging the attitudes of individuals, but although it entails a marked sensitivity to abuses of power (at least as it affects marginalised groups) there is no obvious concern about bureaucratic regimentation which animated the humanists. In adopting this conception of anti-oppressiveness social work/probation has been absorbing and aligning itself with struggles for justice in the wider world. Some of the anti-democratic elements noted by Hall (1994) were absorbed from outside too; others came from social work itself, particularly CCETSW (Webb 1996; Jones 1996, Pinker 1999).

The defining characteristic of the version of anti-oppressiveness developed in social work/probation has been its political and intellectual restrictiveness (see for example, Macey and Moxon, 1996 for an illustration of this in respect of race). It conveyed, as Goldfarb (1999:137) says of its American equivalents, 'formulaic answers that do not address social and political complexity'. Equal opportunity, for example, is exalted within the paradigm as a political principle above all others, a panacea, regardless of context. Access to and opportunity in society are to be worked for regardless of what society itself might be becoming. Deal with racism, sexism, heterosexism, disablism, and ageism, it is implied, and a more convivial world will come into being. Maybe so, but this limited conception of what oppression is and what it means to resist it, leaves a whole series of developments out of the picture: deepening material inequality, the precariousness of work, the increased centralisation of power, the democratic deficit, new surveillance technologies. No coherent account of oppression would omit these developments, which impinge on social work/probation and its clients in very direct ways.

There is not one ingredient of the anti-oppressive paradigm developed by CCETSW in the 1980s and sustained since (uneasily and unevenly) in more than 30 universities, e.g. – its foundation in identity politics (Appiah, 1996), its obsession with difference (Gilroy, 1992), its simplistic understanding of the nature and operation of power and its characterisation of contemporary British society (Modood, 1992) that could not be contested by writers on the liberal Left. It substitutes the idea of categorism for a common universal humanity, in which membership of particular groups and tribes outweighs both shared characteristics (across categories) and individual differences (within categories). It is oblivious, in a way that liberal humanism is not, to the increased likelihood of inter-group hatred occurring – especially ethnic hatred – as a result of an unqualified emphasis on difference, otherness, and categorism (Ignatieff, 1999). In both agencies and academia it has occasionally mocked the very idea of anti-oppressiveness by insisting upon the surveillance of the spoken and written word, disparaging the totalitarian echoes of such speech codes (Goldfarb, 1999; Hall, 1994; Hitchens, 1994). And yet this paradigm has been taught to perhaps a dozen cohorts of social work/probation students as if it were an unquestionable moral orthodoxy, a necessary ingredient of good practice, and the last word on understanding oppression – and despite the availability of other, competing viewpoints elsewhere in civil society, and in academia itself. Despite the recent emergence of a post-modern critique of the 'old' anti-oppressive paradigm (Pease and Fook, 1999), it is still live in the minds of many practitioners and managers who trained since the mid-1980s.

To understand how such an intellectually unsophisticated paradigm took root in social work/probation, and corroded the deliberative traditions of the university programmes with which it was associated, one has to examine the broader policy context in which it developed. Although it is not often remarked upon, it grew in tandem with a shift towards vocationalism in social work/probation training, a move ostensibly intended to tailor training more closely to the 'real world' of agency practice. But this was vocationalism of a particularly debased kind, which I shall call instructionalism, to distinguish it from those forms of professional training which respect and require deliberation and which involve a balance of the intellectual and the practical (Silver and Brennan, 1988). Instructionalism, driven by CCETSW, downplayed the acquisition of bodies of knowledge in favour of practical skills and particular mind-sets allegedly associated with good practice (of which anti-oppressiveness was one), telling students what was required of them. The much vaunted idea of reflective practice in social work training (Fook, 1999) cannot redeem instructionalism if students and trainees are denied the knowledge to reflect with and on.

But a larger question then presents itself. Why did vocationalism take the instructionalist form, when it might have taken one more compatible with the intellectual ideals of a university? The answer lies in the broader managerialist context in which vocationalism itself took shape in the 1980s, which gave expression to a neo-liberal agenda whose hostility to independent centres of professional power was barely disguised (Webb, 1996).

Discouraging deliberation was part of the managerialist intention. Professionalism, however, was challenged in the name of consumerism and service-user empowerment, and the exponents of anti-oppressiveness saw in that strategy an opportunity to advance their own agenda. A once unlikely alliance between radicals and managers, anticipated by McWilliams (1998), came to pass, in which, among other things, attacks on professional discretion were legitimated by discursive links to such noble causes as resisting homophobia and empowering women (because discretion, it was said, was always discriminatory). Later, Pitts (1993:103) noted that anti-racism had become 'a managerially-led "negative" reform' (negative in the sense that it challenged an establishment orthodoxy), while Howe (1994) described the reshaping of several methods of social work intervention to incorporate managerialist – i.e. non-deliberative, instructionalist – models of behavioural change.

Prescient as they were, these early critics did not grasp all the dangers that managerialism represented. It is not an ideologically neutral strategy, not without material consequences of its own. Despite its ascendancy within the public sector, and its apologist's claims to the contrary, it is far from being an unequivocal force for good in social work/probation, even when it threatens bastions of professional (and male, and white) self-interest and privilege. Because of the intricate and intimate way it seeks to control the outlook and behaviour of employees and clients, it can be experienced as a stifling and destructive force, with negative psychological consequences for many who are subject to it (Clemmy, 1998). It could, in fact, be understood as a form of oppression in its own right.

Managerialism and oppression
Managerialism grew from the scientific management strategies developed by Frederick Taylor in the earlier part of the twentieth century, which aimed at increasing productivity (more output for less input) in commercial concerns. This invariably entailed a sharp division of labour, increased standardisation and routinisation of tasks, and, consequentially but not incidentally, greater regimentation of the workforce. As the century progressed various schools of management thought proliferated, all with the same focus on productivity but different views of what it took to achieve it. More recent theories, such as Total Quality Management (which have had more appeal in the public sector), place less overt emphasis on coercive control than Taylorism and more on engineering the consent and motivation of staff. However, as even the more benign academic critics of managerialism admit, elements of the two broad approaches are often entwined in modern workplaces, and the sense of being subject to discipline is never

wholly absent (Newman and Clarke, 1994). The sheer pervasiveness of managerialism in contemporary society – 'the dispersal of "managerial consciousness" across both private and public sector workforces' (Clarke, Cochrane and McLaughlin, 1994: 330) – means that it has 'enormous power [because] large numbers of people are induced or compelled or choose to act in ways that produce and reproduce it' (Hough, 1999:43).

On its own terms managerialism is understood as a way of promoting efficiency, economy and effectiveness in a given organisational context (although in social and political terms it is clearly more than this). The precise way in which managerialisation occurs depends to an extent on the nature of the organisation being subjected to it, but generally it entails an emphasis on pre-set goals and objectives laid down at the top of an organisation, and the integration of all activities within a guiding corporate plan. Organisational hierarchies become flatter, though line management becomes tighter; even if decision making is devolved (say in a geographically dispersed organisation) it is only in terms of how – and how fast – goals and policies laid down at the centre should be achieved. Job specification becomes more precise, broken down into bundles of competences appropriate to particular tasks at particular levels. Clear procedures, protocols, and techniques are laid down – individual discretion is circumscribed. Efficiency is all: computer technologies which speed up the process by which tasks can be accomplished raise psychic expectations of what it is possible to do in a given period, and increase time-pressure on employees. Budgets are tightly controlled, performance-based appraisal and incentive schemes are introduced, backed up with procedures for monitoring outcomes and auditing efficiency.

David Smail, a psychologist, has probed more deeply than most into the existential consequences of managerialism (at least for older workers)

> *If the aim of this managed upheaval in the lives of almost everyone was intended to realise the claims of its superficial rhetoric – that 'time' could be 'managed', for example, it could only be considered a disastrous failure. . . . If on the other hand its actual achievements – of disconcerting, disorienting, and rendering the workforce receptive through sheer vulnerability to the new business ideology – if these were its real intentions, then it was an immense success. The sublime confidence with which [managers] imposed [their] debased language of 'performance indicators', 'Total Quality', and so on, on people who had all their lives spoken, albeit uncritically, a far more ethically nuanced language left them conceptually completely off balance. (Smail, 1993: 106.)*

Even if one discounts the hyperbole in this, it captures some of the painfulness and absurdity of the managerialisation process, the sense that even while it purports to serve some notion of the commercial or public good it diminishes the humanity of the people whose lives are circumscribed by it. Sociologist Richard Sennett (1998) has also explored the effects of management-driven change on the psyche of contemporary workers, concluding that it results in a 'corrosion of character'. Nothing work related is constant enough to invest in; skills are in constant need of updating. Employees are required to be endlessly flexible, to content themselves (if they can) with being little more than units of productivity, implementing policy and nothing more, thinning out their identities and travelling very light in terms of personal commitments. 'Such practices', Sennett (1998:146/148) writes, 'obviously and brutally diminish the sense of mattering as a person, of being necessary to others' and, by sharpening the struggle for individual economic survival, 'provides human beings no deep reasons to care about one another.'

More abstractly, but with the same depth of moral concern, philosopher Charles Taylor has said that the core danger of managerialism

> *is that things that ought to be determined by other criteria will be decided in terms of efficiency or cost-benefit analysis, that the independent ends that ought to be guiding our lives will be eclipsed by the demand to maximise output* (Taylor, 1991;5).

This danger is admittedly recognised, to a degree, even by those who write rather neutrally about managerialism and who believe both that it is possible to distinguish it from 'good management' (which leaves room for independent ends) and that the latter could prevail (Vanstone ,1995). In reality the boundary between the two is much more fragile than is often recognised; in May's (1994) study of local Probation Service decision-making, external (Home Office) pressures to be efficient undermined senior manager's commitment to ideals of good management. Coercion was integral to the process and had to be passed down through the organisation. Commenting on managerialism in criminal justice more generally, Raine and Willson (1993: 220) also recognise the potential for authoritarianism in managerialism, and rather coyly warn against 'compromising our future', while still falling short of calling it a form of oppression.

Nils Christie (1993), however, has gone further, claiming that in the American adult criminal justice system managerial imperatives have already superseded other values, including the values of justice, care, and decency and that the resulting indifference, or amoralism, towards offenders lies behind the high rates of incarceration in that country. Whilst recognising that modern American managerialism has its roots in contemporary capitalism, he discerns within it, with Bauman (1989), the same ethos that fuelled the most extreme form of authoritarianism – totalitarianism – and produced the Holocaust:

> *The conditions for the Holocaust are precisely what has helped to create the industrial society; the division of labour, the modern bureaucracy, the rational spirit, the efficiency, the scientific mentality, and particularly the relegation of values from important sectors of society* (Christie, 1993: 160).

This returns us, alarmingly, to the forgotten concerns of the humanist psychiatrists and political theorists in the aftermath of World War II, and to the idea that perhaps totalitarianism remains, as they believed, an oppression to be feared – 'the most oppressive of nightmares that has haunted our century' (Bauman 1997:17) – and resisted. What I mean by this is expressly not a return to past forms of totalitarianism – Nazism, Fascism, and Communism – but to a new variant of the same political form and its underlying impulse – to centralise, to co-ordinate, to modernise, to regulate, to instruct, to depersonalise, to control debate, to demand allegiance, to restrict freedom – all in the name of a notional public good for which sacrifices of time and liberty must be made. Nor is it to claim that totalitarian tendencies in contemporary Britain (or other western countries) are actually in the ascendant, or that there are no counter-trends or countervailing powers. There are – see Giddens 1999 for claims about the robustness of contemporary western democracy – and indeed, if there were not, it would be pointless making this argument. All that is being claimed here is that totalitarian tendencies and mentalities are in evidence in contemporary managerialism, and that its ethos, reach, and psychic consequences require urgent scrutiny.

In that sense the argument is aligned with philosopher Ernest Gellner (1994:145), who observes sanguinely that 'command-administrative systems [are] the normal condition of humanity' and that democracy (or in his terms, independent civil society) has always to be worked for; with historian Mark Mazower (1998) who has highlighted the precariousness of democratic forms and traditions even in modern Europe; with Ulrich Beck (1992), theorist of 'risk society', who speculates on the possible emergence of a 'legitimate totalitarianism of hazard prevention' (to control crime, for example), and with a long line of social critics who have persistently warned that corporate capitalism is no necessary or even likely guarantor of democratic freedoms (most recently, Hoggart (1999). There is also an obvious point to be made about the contemporary availability of surveillance and information processing technologies that would make new forms of totalitarianism easier to achieve than in the past, and far too little public debate on their use and implications (Norris and Armstrong, 1999).

Conclusion: deliberation and resistance

A large part of what distinguishes democracy from totalitarianism – and of what sustains democracy – is an emphasis on open public deliberation, on the belief that intellectual and ethical enquiry helps to make it possible for a diversity of peoples to understand or at least tolerate each other, to solve complex problems of living, and to coexist. (Goldfarb, 1998). Authoritarian political forms – totalitarianism in particular – are notorious for their anti-intellectualism, for their bias to action, and for making a virtue of hardness (a lack of compassion). The instructionalist ethos of contemporary managerialism – showing people what mind-sets to adopt, limiting the range of required knowledge – is a mild but none the less dismaying analogue of these qualities, a totalitarian milieu in the making. Anything which generates and sustains deliberation, and which wins respect for open and informed dialogue on complex ethical and political issues, weakens authoritarian habits of mind and reduces susceptibility to orthodoxies like the anti-oppressive paradigm.

Once a climate has been established which is hostile to independent-mindedness, 'most of us find our thoughts drawn by a kind of gravitational pull towards the larger mass of Belief around us' (Glover, 1999: 364). It requires courage to go against it. Intellectuals associated with social work/probation, in both universities and agencies, and in the public sphere more generally, must find this courage and insist upon the democratic and professional necessity of deliberation. By going against the orthodoxies they will inevitably be unpopular but, as Goldfarb suggests, there is no better way to unsettle orthodoxies than by provoking talk and thought. It is what intellectuals are for.

In social work/probation, deliberation, whatever instructionalism implies, is never redundant: the quality of client's lives depends on staff thoughtfulness. The knowledge necessary to deliberation is an essential, not an optional, component of what philosopher Jonathan Glover calls 'the moral imagination', a quality much in need of renewal in social work/probation, precisely because it has been so dulled by the narrow range and shallow humanity of the anti-oppressive paradigm. Central to the moral imagination, says Glover,

> *is seeing what is humanly important. When it is stimulated, there is a breakthrough of the human responses, otherwise deadened by such things as distance, tribalism or ideology. It checks conformity and*

> *obedience, bringing to the fore what matters humanly rather than the*
> *current norm or the official policy. It makes vivid the victims and the*
> *human reality of what will be done to them* (Glover, 1999: 409).

The moral imagination can only function if it is nourished by knowledge about developments and possibilities in particular areas of social policy and criminal justice – and by the ability to deliberate ethically upon them. In a penal context, for example, the moral imagination might operate as an important constraint on 'the eliminative ideal' which Rutherford (1998) discerns beneath so much contemporary penal policy. It informs Vivian Sterns (1998) insistence that prisoners, banished behind bars and walls, are still people, and that the opening of new prisons now, especially private ones, is 'a sin against the future', because what we build, we shall use. It informs Norris and Armstrong's (1999) fears that the expansion of CCTV may have negative consequences that outweigh its short term impact as a means of reducing crime.

There are no good reasons why probation officers (and trainees), for example, as one among several types of expert in crime control, should not be expected to learn and think about these things, and be prepared, when the occasion demands, to enter into public debate about them. If not them, who? If addressing such issues is not about addressing oppression – and judged both by the available textbooks and the everyday discourse of trainers and educators in social work/probation terms it is not – one must inevitably be wary of the motives of those who have defined the term 'oppression' so narrowly.

The instructionalist version of vocationalism that has come to dominate social work/ probation training – the version most compatible with managerialism – does not require or encourage thinking about such matters, because, superficially at least, they are not relevant to the demands of immediate face-to-face practice with offenders. They may, incidentally, be touched on by teachers with a particular interest in them, but they are in no sense requirements. Even though perfectly sound material for deliberation may be produced elsewhere in universities, and may even have been produced with educated practitioners in mind (much criminological literature, for example), it would find no necessary place on social work/probation training courses.

There is every reason for universities to be involved in vocational training for a broad range of occupations, but not if the model of such training deliberately precludes deliberation, in the way that instructionalism does. The only possible justification for involving universities is to do what they are best at doing, and remain best at doing, even in the era of cyberspace and information technology, and that is creating a gathering place and providing the resources for systematic deliberation to occur (Kumar, 1999). There are other bodies in society that can easily compete with the university as providers of mere instruction (although no others have the same prestige or the powers of accreditation) but none that can – and usually still do – cultivate the virtues of knowledgeability, analysis, argument, and imagination to quite the same extent. (Smith and Webster, 1997: 108).

There are, of course, two difficulties with this claim. Firstly, such qualities have already, and quite easily, been rendered less important by the instructionalist emphasis on social work/probation courses, and for all their ideals of intellectual freedom and social responsibility, universities have been very variable in attempting to resist this (Pinker, 1999). There is, after all, money at stake. Secondly, and perhaps more importantly, it is widely recognised that the entire British university system is now starting to experience the same managerial, vocational revolution that began specifically for social work in the 1980s, with the same overall emphasis on objective setting, targets, performance indicators, budget control, centralisation of institutional authority, loss of professional discretion, and erosion of viable humanistic traditions of learning and teaching (Melody, 1997). There are widespread anxieties about the broader social and institutional consequences of this, and already concern has been expressed about 'the Taylorisation of intellectual labour in academia' (Dominelli and Hoogveldt, 1996). There is still room for manoeuvre here, but mostly the need for courageous people – who resist 'every manifestation of impersonal power that claims to be beyond good and evil, anywhere and everywhere, no matter how it disguises its tricks and manifestations' (Havel, 1991: 268) – is made more urgent.

References
Appiah K (1996) 'Race, Culture, Identity' in Appiah K A and Gutmann A *Colour Conscious: The Political Morality of Race* Princeton, Princeton University

Bauman Z (1989) *Modernity and the Holocaust* Cambridge, Polity

Bauman Z (1997) *Postmodernity and its Discontents* Cambridge, Polity

Beck U (1992) *Risk society* London, Sage

Bettleheim B (1960) *The Informed Heart: Autonomy in a Mass Age* New York, Avon Books

Briskman L and Noble C (1999) 'Social Work Ethics: embracing diversity?' in Pease B and Fook J (eds) *Transforming Social Work Practice: postmodern critical perspectives* London, Routledge

Clarke J, Cochrane A and McLaughlin E (1994) 'Mission Accomplished or Unfinished Business?' The impact of managerialisation' in Clarke J, Cochrane A and McLaughlin E (eds) *Managing Social Policy* London, Sage

Christie N (1993) *Crime Control as Industry: towards gulags western-style?* London, Routledge

Clemmy T (1998) *Stress in the Probation Service* ACOP/Manchester University

Dominelli L and Hoogveldt A (1996) 'Globalisation, Contract Government and the Taylorisation of Intellectual Labour in Academia Studies' in *Political Economy* 49 (Spring)

Douglas A (1999) 'Political Correctness: Myth or Reality?' in Philpot T (ed) *Political Correctness and Social Work* London, Institute of Economic Affairs

Fook J (1999) 'Critical Reflexivity in Education and Practice' in Pease B and Fook J (eds) *Transforming Social Work Practice: postmodern critical perspectives* London, Routledge

Gellner, E (1994) *Conditions of Liberty: civil society and its rivals* Hamondsworth, Penguin

Giddens A (1999) *Runaway world: how globalisation is shaping our lives* London, Profile Books

Gilroy P (1992) 'The End of Anti-Racism' in Donald J and Ratansi A (eds) *Race' Culture and Difference* London, Sage

Glover J (1999) *Humanity: The Moral History of the Twentieth Century* London, Jonathan Cape

Goldfarb J C (1998) *Civility and Diversion: the intellectual in democratic society* Cambridge, Cambridge University Press

Hall S (1994) 'Some 'Politically Incorrect' Pathways through PC' in Dunant S (ed.) *The War of the Words: The political correctness debate* London, Virago

Havel V (1991) 'Politics and Conscience' in Wilson P (ed.) *Vaclav Havel – Open Letters: selected prose 1965-1999* London, Faber and Faber

Hitchens C (1994) The Fraying of America: a review of 'Culture of Complaint' by Robert Hughes in Dunant S (ed) *The War of the Words: The political correctness debate* London, Virago

Hoggart R (1999) *First and Last things* London, Aurum Press

Hough G (1999) 'The Organisation of Social Work in the Customer Culture' in Pease B and Fook J (eds) *Transforming Social Work Practice: postmodern critical perspectives* London, Routledge

Howe D (1994) 'Knowledge, Power and Social Work Methods' in Davies M (ed.) *The Sociology of Social Work* London, Routledge

Hugman R and Smith D (1995) An overview: in Hugman R and Smith D (eds) *Ethical Issues in Social Work* London, Routledge

Ignatieff M (1999) *The Warrior's Honour: Ethnic War and the Modern Conscience*.London, Vintage

Jones C (1996) 'Anti-intellectualism and the Peculiarities of British Social Work Education' in Parton N (ed.) *Social Theory, Social Change and Social Work* London, Routledge

Kumar K (1999) 'The Need for Place' in Smith A and Webster F (eds) *The Postmodern University? contested visions of higher education in society* Buckingham, Open University Press

Macy M and Moxon E (1996) An Examination of Anti-Racist and Anti-Oppressive Theory and Practice in Social Work Education *British Journal of Social Work* 26

Marsh P and Triseliotis J (1997) *Ready to Practice* Aldershot, Arena, Practice

May T (1994) Transformative Power: a study in a human service organisation *The Sociological Review* 42(4)

Mazower M (1998) *Dark Continent: Europe's twentieth century* Harmondsworth, Penguin

McWilliams W (1988) Probation, Pragmatism and Policy in *Howard Journal* 26(2)

Melody W (1997) 'Universities and Public Policy' in Smith A and Webster F (eds) *The Postmodern University? contested visions of higher education in society* Buckingham, Open University Press

Modood T (1992) 'British Asian Muslims and the Rushdie Affair' in Donald J and Ratansi A (eds) *Race' Culture and Difference* London, Sage

Newman J and Clarke J (1994) 'Going About Our Business: The Managerialisation of Public Services' in Clarke J, Cochrane A and McLaughlin E (ed.) *Managing Social Policy* London Sage

Norris C and Armstrong G (1999) *The Maximum Surveillance Society: The rise of CCTV* Oxford, Berg

Pearson G (1975) 'Making Social Workers: bad promises and good omens' in Bailey R and Brake M (eds) *Radical Social Work* London, Edward Arnold

Pease B and Fook J (1999) *Transforming Social Work Practice: postmodern critical perspectives* London: Routledge

Pinker R (1999) 'Social Work and Adoption: A Case of Mistaken Identities' in Philpot T (ed.) *Political Correctness and Social Work* London Institute of Economic Affairs

Pitts J (1993) 'Thereotyping: Anti-Racism, Criminology and Black Young People' in Cook D and Hudson B (eds) *Racism and criminology* London, Sage

Raine J W and Willson M J (1993) *Managing Criminal Justice* London: Harvester Wheatsheaf

Rutherford A (1998) 'Crime Policy and the Eliminative Ideal' in Jones-Finer C and Nellis M (eds) *Crime and Social Exclusion* Oxford, Blackwell

Sennett R (1998) *The Corrosion of Character: The personal consequences of work in the new capitalism* New York, W W Norton and Co

Sliver H and Brennan J (1988) *A Liberal Vocationalism* London, Methuen

Smail D (1993) *The Origins of Unhappiness: a new understanding of personal distress* London, Harper Collins

Smith A and Webster F (1997) 'Conclusion: An Affirming Flame' in Smith A and Webster F (eds) *The Postmodern University? contested visions of higher education in society* Buckingham, Open University Press

Stern V (1998) *A Sin Against the Future; imprisonment in the world* Harmondsworth: Penguin

Stuart-Hughes H (1975) *The Sea Change: The Migration of Social Thought 1930-1965* London, Harper and Row

Taylor C (1991) *The Ethics of Authenticity* London, Harvard University Press

Vanstone M (1995) 'Managerialism and the Ethics of Management' in Hugman R and Smith D (eds) *Ethical Issues in Social Work* London, Routledge

Webb D (1996) 'Regulation for Radicals: The State, CCETSW and the Academy' in Parton N (ed) *Social Theory, Social Change and Social Work* London, Routledge

Younghusband, E (1978) *Social Work in Britain 1950-1975: A Follow-Up Study Vol II* London, George Allen and Unwin

Chapter 5
Accountability and Social Work Research
Jackie Powell

The nature of social work itself remains a highly contested area as, throughout its history, it has been continually influenced by dominant political ideas. As Lorenz (1994) notes:

> *'Traditionally, social work's place and function in society centres on the creation of internal social peace, to be established not primarily by coercive means but through the considered, informed and professional negotiation of differences and inequalities. Social work has a "dual mandate" for these negotiations, from individuals and from society at large either through state agencies or through non-governmental organisations. It was originally not just a private, charitable movement but an organised, systematic activity which took account of the overall societal context in which it operated and developed' (p.4).*

Social work, then, is not a neutral activity; rather, moral and political issues lie at its heart (Hugman and Smith 1995). Whilst being invited to intervene in highly complex human situations, social workers are increasingly expected to provide straightforward solutions. In this context, social work has become the subject of scrutiny and its effectiveness questioned. Alternatively conceived as a set of skills and competencies, a pragmatic approach to problem solving or a political activity directed towards change, social work faces an uncertain future (Parton 1996).

Social workers, however, are not alone in being asked to account for their activities. Over the past decade or more there has been an unprecedented growth in evaluation and evaluation bodies as successive governments have attempted to control public expenditure and implant a new managerial culture in the public sector. As Henkel (1991) has argued, evaluation of public sector services has become an essential prerequisite of effective accountability and significant change. Barritt (1994) identifies a similar trend in the voluntary sector where there is increasing emphasis on the development of management information systems and performance measurement. He identifies the need for what he calls a 'more pluralistic and creative evaluation culture for the next century' which encourages a more open approach to the collection, discussion, and interpretation of information, rather than limiting it to a narrowly defined range of outcome measures. However, where the phenomenon of multiple stakeholders in evaluation has been acknowledged, it has frequently been used as a means of weakening the control over evaluation previously thought to be held by providers and, in particular, professional providers (Henkel, 1998). Service users may have an input, although the dominant evaluative voice remains essentially management-orientated with users' views being framed as consumer feedback (Barnes 1994). Not surprisingly, there is a growing emphasis within many evaluative studies on accountability expressed in terms of cost effectiveness of public monies coupled with attention to service users' views. This dual accountability is also evident in the challenges faced by social workers in their day-to-day practice, where they work with a multiplicity of interests and competing demands from what Clarke (1994) calls 'the top down' and 'the margins'.

The reconciliation of the possible conflicting interests of the wider public for a careful utilisation of resources with the individual's needs for an accessible and responsive service raises a range of significant questions about the nature of accountability between professional and manager, and professional and service user. Given this multiplicity of interests, accountability emerges as a highly contested concept, where political, financial, professional, and user concerns compete in their demands for recognition and primacy. Existing links of accountability have become overloaded, broken or obscured and there is now a need to develop new forms of linkage which acknowledge some of the tensions inherent in public sector accountability. As Day and Klein (1987) identified over a decade ago:

> *Accountability is not merely seen as a crucial link in the chain between governors and governed: effective democracy, it is argued, implies a system which ensures that the former are accountable to the latter. Equally accountability is increasingly seen as a means of stretching scare resources; if better value for money is to be achieved in the public sector, it is argued, then once again an effective system of accountability is needed* (p.1).

Accountability, then, takes multiple forms for those engaged in planning, managing, and delivering services and the task for those in the public sector, or in the independent sector taking on the role of public service, becomes one of balancing those accountabilities (James 1994). Financial accountability (to funders) has to operate within a wider remit of these other accountabilities: accountability to (potential) users to meet identified need, to professionals to enable them to practise effectively, to politicians to ensure implementation of their policies, and to managers to ensure the organisational goals are achieved.

Focusing on accountability as multi-dimensional, this paper examines the need for an approach to research and evaluation in social work which acknowledges this multiplicity of interests and seeks to employ methods for promoting the inclusion of these several interested parties in the research process. First, it explores the different frameworks adopted in social work research and then goes on to explore in more detail those approaches which recognise the plurality of interests and perspectives in social work practice. It concludes with some discussion of the implications for the researcher in adopting an approach which involves people in dialogue and debate directed towards achieving a shared understanding as a basis for change.

The nature of the relationship between social work and research has been and continues to be a much disputed issue in the UK. Whilst there is general agreement that social work research has a contribution to make towards effective practice, questions remain as to the nature of social work itself and what constitutes effective practice. Many early pioneers of social work saw themselves as part of the great reformist tradition of the late nineteenth and early twentieth centuries and were closely associated with the work of social researchers at that time (Finch, 1986). With the emergence of professional bodies modelled on the more established professions, most notably medicine, the emphasis shifted towards the development of expert knowledge and skills and a research tradition reflecting this influence. For example, the use of experiment and quasi-experimental design to examine the effectiveness of social work practice has been well documented by Sheldon (1986). As the development of ideas and practices in social work has evolved, so too have the debates over the appropriate use of different approaches to research in social work (see, for example, Sheldon, 1984; Raynor, 1984; Smith, 1987).

In a recent paper by Liz Trinder (1996) entitled *Social Work Research: the state of the art (or science)* three major schools of social work research are identified. First, empirical practice and experiment, where randomised controlled trials are seen as the gold standard (see MacDonald and Sheldon, 1992). Second, pragmatism and partnership, characterised by an eclectic approach to research methodology and an acknowledgement of the presence of a multiplicity of perspectives (see Cheetham *et al.*, 1992). Finally, participatory or critical research where the emphasis is on the political and potentially empowering role of research (see Everitt and Hardiker, 1996). Shaw's work on mapping the range of methodologies adopted in social work evaluation identifies similar broad approaches (Shaw and Shaw, 1997).

While all these approaches recognise, to varying degrees, the plurality of interests and perspectives, and not least in the fields of social and health care, there has been a resurgence of the randomised controlled trial as the gold standard of evaluative practice in the eyes of research commissioners, regardless of whether the evaluation concerns a new drug or an organisational development. For example, substantial public resources have been devoted to such initiatives as the current NHS Research and Development Strategy, where the emphasis is on evidence-based practice and clinical effectiveness. A similar trend in social work research is also gaining ground with the setting up of the Centre for Evidence-Based Social Services (CEBSS) at the University of Exeter. One part of the Centre's brief is to encourage practitioners to make more use of the research that currently exists and to support and promote new research that is focused on outcomes. As the Director of the Centre states:

> . . . *the need to carefully monitor and report upon service outcomes is now firmly on political, managerial and professional agendas – as exemplified by the existence of the Exeter Centre* (Sheldon 1998: p.17).

The Centre is firmly focused on promoting studies of effectiveness 'screened for methodological adequacy', where the use of positivistic methods of scientific research is explicitly favoured (MacDonald and Sheldon 1992).

This privileging of empirical practice and experiment has been criticised by a number of writers engaged in health and social care research for its attempt to impose a rational, scientific framework on what is in reality a messy, value-laden activity (Hunter, 1998). In social work, this type of approach has often been regarded with distrust by professional practitioners for a number of reasons. In part this reflects an unease with a research paradigm where there is a premium on evaluations rooted in a positivist methodology, focusing on what might loosely be described as the measurable and quantifiable. This approach, which objectifies people and processes, sits ill with conceptions of reflective practice and research as critical enquiry (Harrison and Humphreys 1997). This distrust of such an approach also reflects a wariness (and weariness) of the management culture and its preoccupation with performance indicators, quality standards and cost-effectiveness studies. Shaw and Shaw (1997), in their recent study of evaluation practices, highlight such concerns on the part of social workers and probation officers, who distinguished between 'evaluation proper' and 'self-evaluation'. The former was undertaken as part of the management of the service and served the interests of the agency in focusing on quantifiable aspects of performance and service quality. In contrast to this approach, self-evaluation was much more concerned with engaging with service users and making use of qualitative methods of enquiry to explore the various perceptions of the service.

A more open approach to the use of a wide range of research methods and the acknowledgement of multiple perspectives within the research process is what Trinder (1996) refers to as pragmatism and partnership. It is characterised by an eclectic approach to research methodology and attention to views and experiences of both practitioners and service users. Much of the work which might be included under this heading has been undertaken as part of the programme of DoH-commissioned research, now drawn together in 'Messages From Research' (DoH,1995). This publication reports on findings drawn from these studies in ways designed to inform policy makers and professionals involved in protecting children. Thus, this type of research can be seen as making a contribution towards effective practice. At the same time, there is an acknowledgement of different perspectives on what might constitute effective practice and who might be involved in this debate (Little 1998).

Over a number of years, many of those engaged in the evaluation of health and social care services have sought to make explicit the diversity of perspectives on what constitutes the effectiveness of a service or practice. For example, attention to user-orientated issues such as accessibility and responsiveness to individual needs was evident a decade or more ago in Smith and Cantley's (1985) study of a psychogeriatric hospital. Central to the design of the study was an acknowledgement that such services meet a variety of interests, possibly conflicting in their views of what might constitute a successful service. In giving attention to the viewpoints of all stakeholder groups this pluralistic approach usefully opens up the complexity of defining both success and effectiveness. It also offers the opportunity to identify the ways in which competing interests jockey for position and a voice to be heard. By identifying these different interests and the potential connections between them, not least issues of power imbalance between the various parties, it offers the opportunity for a wider debate about service planning and delivery, rather than any clear way forward for either policy makers or practitioners. This can be seen as its potential strength – there are no definitive answers to questions such as 'How effective are our services?'

However, given today's greater preoccupation with public accountability amid resource constraint there is a need for some consideration of issues of costs alongside this diversity of views on service objectives and performance. An example of an interdisciplinary study which sought to acknowledge the importance of costs alongside the views of the several 'interested parties' was work undertaken by myself and a colleague from Management Science (Powell and Goddard 1996). An important feature of this study was the setting up of a stakeholder representatives' group whose membership included representatives from all the principal groups of stakeholders: managers, different professional groups (medicine, social work, nursing, and occupational therapy), a representative from the voluntary sector, a general practitioner, a carer, and a patient advocate. The group initially provided a forum for the discussion of data collected from stakeholder interviews. Later, it formed the main source of stakeholder views for the planning of the future service.

The group proved successful in ensuring that a wide range of views were taken into consideration and offered the opportunity for discussion and debate. It provided a forum for some parties, who previously had had limited information and little involvement in the development of the service, to challenge the various professionals' perspectives. The involvement of a carer and a patient advocate (representing older people with mental health problems as primary users of the service) was also important in addressing the different experiences and perspectives of direct users and carers. However, the built-in inequalities of power among the various participants remained largely unchallenged, although they were acknowledged to the extent that one of the principal researchers acted as chair of the group and attempted at all times to facilitate a wide discussion involving all members. During the period of the project the balance of power between the medical consultants and general managers shifted in favour of the latter. This was in the context of a wider shift from professionalism to managerialism. Although at times alliances were formed between the managers and professionals, areas of conflict around the management of resources and accountability became more evident over time. However, the involvement of a wide membership within the group tended to limit this 'jockeying' for position, which might otherwise have become a major preoccupation and distraction for all parties.

There are a number of lessons to be drawn from this study. To some extent, it was successful in promoting wider participation and debate among a range of interested parties, including some not previously involved in the process of service planning and delivery. In doing so, it promoted a more democratic approach to evaluation in the contemporary context of social and health care. Its success, however, was short-lived. Managers and professionals supported the project throughout but the stakeholders group remained highly dependent on the research project. Once the project ended (and the research report completed), despite the express wishes of the group to continue, it did not do so. To sustains this type of approach requires substantial commitment on the part of the organisation and a recognition of the (potential) benefits which might accrue from having a plurality of stakeholder views set alongside information costs. It also raises issues concerning the role of the researcher and the extent to which he/she becomes an active participant in the process of change, not least in an organisational context.

The model of the researcher as actively engaged in a process of collaboration in bringing about change is a key feature of what Trinder (1996) identifies as participatory or critical research; here the emphasis is on the political nature of research and its potentially empowering role. Rather than retaining the role of expert with overall control of research methodology, including the presentation of an 'overview of perspectives', the researcher is required to move beyond partnership and adopt an emancipatory stance. For example, in the field of poverty research, Bob Holman (1987) argues that the majority of work undertaken in this area is 'about, on or for the poor, not by or with the poor' (p.670). This view is strongly echoed by other writers who have drawn attention to the exploitative nature of research which seeks the active involvement of research subjects in the research process, but fails to confront the inequalities of power at whatever level they occur (see, for example Stanley and Wise 1983; Oliver 1992). The importance of this shift lies, as Reason (1988) argues:

> . . . *in establishing a dialogue between research workers and grass roots people with whom they work, in order to discover and realise the practical and cultural needs of those people* (p.2).

Such an approach, whilst initially attractive in relation to its emancipatory stance and its challenging of oppression, raises issues concerning the extent to which the role of the researcher involves advocacy. For example, in the well-established tradition of client-based research studies, the extent to which primacy is given to service users' views remains a highly contested area. In arguing strongly for prominence being given to service users' evaluations, Wallace and Rees (1988) make explicit their own view that 'social workers' responsibility is never to lose sight of the needs of the most powerless people'. However, an uncritical 'consumerist' approach does not necessarily promote service users' interests. Service users frequently express low expectations about the availability and quality of services and, as Sainsbury (1987) warns, it is important for the researcher to ensure that these evaluations are not simply used as a way of rationing services or maintaining the *status quo*. Rather, the task of the researcher, like the social worker, is to ensure that these voices are heard and understood in the context of often-competing concerns and interests and inequalities of power.

From this overview of approaches to research and evaluation in social work and social care, it is evident that each takes account of the context in which the research gets conducted in different ways. In part, this is reflected in the extent to which the plurality of perspectives and interests within social work policy and practice are acknowledged and addressed within the research process. If the intention is for research to have an impact, to make a difference, then it is essential for the researcher to have an understanding of this wider context and multiplicity of interests, and to work with these several potential users of research in ways which are of mutual benefit. Research activity in social work is increasingly judged by its relevance to a wide range of users and the ways in which both practitioners and service users are engaged in the research process (Cheetham and Deakin 1997). This is entirely appropriate given the nature and purpose of social work and social care services. At the same time it adds to the complexity of the task and raises issues of accountability for the researcher which, in many respects, mirror those of the social worker. It also raises a fundamental question about the exclusivity of the researcher's role as expert in methods of data collection, analysis, and interpretation. Is it possible, or even appropriate some might argue, to seek to reconcile these often conflicting demands on the researcher to act in the interests of those identified as least powerful and to ensure adequate attention to theoretical and methodological issues underpinning the research practice itself?

Several writers, especially those seeking a more explicit advocacy role for the researcher, have argued for the highest priority being given to the participation of members of oppressed groups (Lather 1991). Others have urged caution in adopting such an explicitly political approach as it could be seen to be abandoning the researcher's obligation to maintain an objective standpoint (Hammersley 1995). In her critique of this debate, Humphries (1997) highlights the need for careful scrutiny of both traditional and emancipatory approaches in the making of their knowledge claims and argues the need for self-reflexivity on the part of the researcher. The principle of reflexivity, alternatively described as the acknowledgement of the human dynamic in the research process, continues to be a much contested topic in research, although strongly and persuasively argued by many researchers (Steier 1991). In the context of promoting increased participation in the research process, it can be seen as crucially important. With the recognition of a multiplicity of interests, researchers may find themselves in a complex web of differing perspectives, each of which demands attention.

Mindful of the multiple accountabilities identified within the social work and social care context, what is argued here is a research approach which seeks to identify the several different constituent groups, and attends to the ways in which they are able to marshal power and resources to pursue their interests (and at what costs to other groups). This opens up the way for establishing dialogue. Certain groups can be assisted or supported in pursuit of their inclusion in the research process, not least those whose interests have been denied or received, until relatively recently, insufficient attention, especially users, carers, and other less powerful groups.

By way of illustration, I want to refer briefly to an example in the specific context of evaluating services, where attention to a diversity of views was central to the understanding of the different experiences of a number of interested parties. The focus of this study was evaluating UK participation in a European disability programme where, it was argued, the involvement and views of disabled people had to take a central place, given that the programme itself aimed to promote the full participation of disabled people in society (Powell and Lovelock 1997). This does not appear, in any way, to be contentious. However, establishing the need to set the views of disabled people (primarily although not exclusively as service users) alongside those of policy makers and front-line practitioners in the research process required considerable negotiation on the part of the researchers before agreement was reached. Issues of accountability were raised in relation to the funding of the programme, the purpose of involving professionals in networking in the European context and the appropriateness of extending participation in the programme's activities to disabled people. In many ways the involvement of disabled people in the research study was more extensive than their involvement in the programme and reflected the researchers' views of their own multiple accountabilities, in this context. Even so, it must be acknowledged that disabled people were not actively involved in the initial planning and design of the study (Oliver 1992). Subsequent studies in this field, however, have sought increased participation of disabled people in the research process.

Conceived as an interactive participatory practice, much depends on the ways in which the researcher makes use of negotiating skills in managing the diverse and often conflicting interests inherent in the task. In drawing on two examples from my own research practice, it is evident that skills in negotiation can be employed to identify different interests and facilitate participation. However, negotiations, whilst successful in engaging a wide range of potential participants, may not necessarily lead to their active involvement in dialogue as a basis for shared learning and achieving change (Rees 1991). Attention has to be given to those voices previously unheard or dismissed on the basis that all participants have expertise and knowledge to share. Such an approach establishes the researcher in the role of facilitator, who also has expertise to share but, unlike more traditional approaches, is not expected to produce the definitive account of reality. By playing a key role in challenging rather than re-enforcing in-built power structures the researcher becomes engaged in shifting the process of participation beyond co-operation and consultation towards greater collaboration and co-learning (Reason 1994).

The extent to which this inclusionary approach is sustained will depend on the ways in which the researcher seeks to include these multiple interests throughout the research process: in defining the research question and the overall research methodology, as well as the more specific use of research methods. When research is conceived in this way it involves rather more than the relatively straightforward application of techniques of data collection and analysis. Whilst a continuous re-examination of the relative merits of different research methods and techniques is part of this process, it is not a simple matter of deciding between quantitative and qualitative methods. It is important to remember that all methods have the potential to exploit research participants, including the researcher. For example, Finch (1993) draws attention to the potentially exploitative nature of qualitative interviewing of women. Moreover, traditional survey methods, as Hakim (1988) suggests, may have something to commend them because of their transparency. Given the importance attached to 'interpretation of subjective meaning, description of social context, and attention to lay knowledge' as criteria of good qualitative health research (Popay *et al.*, 1998), and equally applicable in social care and social work research, an appropriate emphasis might be placed on the value of qualitative data. However, the use of quantitative methods or data is thereby neither excluded nor privileged. Careful consideration needs to be given to the way in which any method is used. For example, this might involve the researcher in making explicit, in a way as jargon free as possible, both the value and limitation of any particular method, as well as its likely impact on those involved. Some methods, mostly qualitative in nature, offer greater opportunities for interaction between the researcher and the researched. This may also open up a more active consideration of alternative methods and ways of involving some groups, previously excluded from research, in having 'a voice' as respondents and, as some studies have shown, the opportunity to influence the research agenda by becoming directly involved in data collection and analysis (Whitmore 1994).

To conclude: the main purpose of this paper has been to offer an account of how social work research and evaluation might adopt an approach congruent with social work's commitment to empowerment and inclusionary practices, whilst at the same time taking account of a diversity of interests within social work and, relatedly, social work research. Negotiating skills, it is argued, are important in promoting a wider participation of all parties throughout the research process and in ensuring adequate discussion of research methodology and greater transparency in the use of all research methods, regardless of their conventional or innovative nature.

The importance of pursuing such an approach lies in its ability to promote and facilitate dialogue between all participants, rather than perpetuating the interests of some whilst excluding others from this activity. However, to promote this sort of dialogue and debate there has to be a willingness to acknowledge differences of view and a preparedness to be influenced by others, coupled with an underlying belief in the possibility and value of 'dialogic communication' as a basis for making knowledge claims. Such issues remain hotly contested in theory and practice, although there are some grounds for cautious optimism that such an approach opens up possibilities of new understandings and change previously seen as impossible (Blaug 1994;1995). Social work research, like social work itself, needs to address the complexities of accountability and explore different ways of engaging with research participants as a basis for generating shared understanding and forms of knowledge relevant to practice. Herein lies the contribution that research can make to 'social work making a difference'.

References
Barnes, M (1994) 'Objective science or social interaction? Researching users' views of services' *Research, Policy and Planning* 12(2), pp 1-3

Blaug, R (1994) 'Habermas' treatment for relativism' *Politics* 14(2), pp 51-7

Blaug, R (1995) 'Distortion of the face to face: Communicative reason and social work' British Journal of Social Work 25(4), pp 423-39

Barritt, A (1994) 'Contract culture or anarchy? Evaluation and the voluntary sector' *Research, Policy and Planning* 11(1/2), pp 10-16

Cheetham, J and Deakin, N (1997) 'Research note assessing the assessment: some reflections on the 1996 Higher Education Funding Council's Research Assessment Exercise' *British Journal of Social Work* 27(3), pp 435-42

Cheetham, J, Fuller, R, McIvor,G and Petch, A (1992) *Evaluating Social Work Effectiveness* Buckingham, Open University Press

Clarke, J (ed.) (1994) *A Crisis in Care? Challenges to Social Work* Buckingham, Open University Press

Day, P and Klein, R (1987) *Accountabilities: five public sector services* London, Tavistock

Department of Health (1995) *Child Protection: Messages from Research. Studies in Child Protection* London, HMSO

Everitt, A and Hardiker, P (1996) *Evaluating for Good Practice* London, Macmillan

Finch, J (1993) 'It's great to have someone to talk to: ethics and politics of interviewing women' in Hammersley, M (ed.) *Social Research: Philosophy, Politics and Practice* London, Sage, pp 166-80

Finch, J (1986) *Research and Policy: the uses of qualitative methods in social and educational research* Lewes, Sussex, Falmer Press

Hakim, C (1988) Research Design London, Unwin Hyman

Hammersley, M (1995) *The Politics of Social Research* London, Sage

Harrison, C and Humphreys, C (1997) Keeping Research in Mind, London, Central Council for Education and Training in Social Work

Henkel, M (1998) *Professional Practice: Alternative conceptions of education and evaluation* Southampton, Centre for Evaluative and Developmental Research, Department of Social Work Studies, University of Southampton

Henkel, M (1991) 'The New Evaluative State' *Public Administration* 69, pp 121-36

Holman, B (1987) 'Research From the Underside' *British Journal of Social Work* 17(6), pp 669-83

Hugman, R and Smith, D (1995) *Ethical Issues in Social Work* London, Routledge

Humphries, B (1997) 'From critical thought to emancipatory action: contradictory research goals?' *Sociological Research Online* 2(1) http://www.socresonline. org.uk/socresonline/2/1/3.html

Hunter, D (1998) 'The New Health Policy Agenda: The challenge facing managers and researchers' Research, Policy and Planning 16(2), pp 2-6

James, A (1994) *Managing To Care: Public Sector and the Market* London, Longman

Lather, P (1991) *Getting Smart: Feminist Research and Pedagogy with/in the Postmodern* London, Routledge

Little, M (1998) 'Whispers in the library: A response to Liz Trinder's article on the state of social work research' *Child and Family Social Work* 3, pp 49-56

Lorenz, W (1994) *Social Work in a Changing Europe* London, Routledge

MacDonald, G and Sheldon, B (1992) 'Contemporary studies of the effectiveness of social work' *British Journal of Social Work* 22(6), pp 614-43

Oliver, M (1992) 'Changing the Social Relations of Research Production', *Disability Handicap and Society* 7(2), pp 101-15

Parton, N (ed.) (1996) *Social Theory, Social Change and Social Work* London, Routledge

Popay, J, Rogers, A and Williams, G (1998) 'Rationale and standards for the systematic review of qualitative literature in health services research' *Qualitative Health Research* 8(3), pp 341-51

Powell, J and Goddard, A (1996) 'Cost and stakeholder views: a combined approach to evaluating services' *British Journal of Social Work* 26(1), pp 93-108

Powell, J and Lovelock, R (1997) 'Participants or recipients – disabled people's involvement in a european programme' *British Journal of Social Work* 27(4), pp 565-83

Raynor, P (1984) 'Evaluation with one eye closed: the empiricist agenda in social work' *British Journal of Social Work* 14(1), pp 1-10

Reason, P (ed.) (1988) *Human Inquiry in Action: developments in new paradigm research* London, Sage

Reason, P (ed.) (1994) *Participation in Human Enquiry* London, Sage

Rees, S (1991) *Achieving Power: practice and policy in social welfare* Sydney, Australia, Allen and Unwin

Sainsbury, E (1987) 'Client studies: their contribution and limitations in influencing social work practice' *British Journal of Social Work* 17(6), pp 635-44

Shaw, I and Shaw, A (1997) 'Keeping social work honest: evaluating as profession and practice' *British Journal of Social Work* 27(6), pp 847-69

Sheldon, B (1984) 'Evaluation with one eye closed: the empiricist agenda in social work – a reply to Peter Raynor' *British Journal of Social Work* 14(6), pp 635-7

Sheldon, B (1986) 'Social work effectiveness experiments: review and implications' British Journal of Social Work 16(2), pp 223-42

Sheldon, B (1998) 'Evidence-based social services: prospects and problems' *Research, Policy and Planning* 16(2), pp 16-18

Smith, D (1987) 'The Limits of Positivism in Social Work Research' *British Journal of Social Work* 17(4), pp 573-86

Smith, G and Cantley, C (1985) *Assessing Health Care: A study in organisational evaluation* Milton Keynes, Open University Press

Stanley, L and Wise, S (1983) *Breaking Out: Feminist Consciousness and Feminist Research* London, Routledge and Kegan Hall

Steier, F (ed.) (1991) *Research and Reflexivity* London, Sage

Trinder, L (1996) 'Social work research: the state of the art (or science)' *Child and Family Social Work* 1, pp 233-42

Wallace, E and Rees, S (1988) 'The priority of client evaluations' in Lishman, J (ed.) *Evaluation. Research Highlights in Social Work, 8 2nd ed.* London, Jessica Kingsley Publishers, pp 58-71

Whitmore, E (1994) 'To tell the truth: working with oppressed groups in participatory approaches to inquiry' in Reason, P (ed.) *Participation in Human Inquiry* London, Sage, pp 82-98

Chapter 6
Revaluing Professional Social Work Assessment
Derek Clifford

Introduction

The object of this chapter is to assert the possibility of a theoretical framework for social work assessment within the context of the recent consensus that there *is* no such thing and no agreement on what it might be, and widespread undervaluing and lack of respect for social work assessment. What is presented here aims to critically revalue what professional social work at its best has always tried to do. It suggests that social work, despite its late-twentieth-century critics, is well placed to 'make a difference' in the new millennium, and that there are good enough grounds for suggesting that contemporary social theory and social work practice can offer an intellectual framework that is *at least as convincing and valid as theoretical frameworks offered by other professions*. What it has to offer in terms of social assessment should therefore be offered with confidence, and defended as a crucial element in any multi-professional assessment arena.

It is not presented as an unsupported or merely theoretical innovation. The framework has been discussed and co-researched with experienced social work practitioners in child protection training jointly organised with social services training officers and child protection co-ordinators. It has also been developed in relation to earlier research into adoption and fostering practices in assessment in voluntary and statutory settings, and has also been presented and discussed at a research conference on community care with older people.

The 'missing' theoretical framework for social assessment

The psychiatrist Peter Reder has made significant contributions to the area of child protection assessment in recent years (Reder, Duncan and Gray, 1993, and Reder and Lucey, 1995), and in the introductory chapter to the 1995 edited work on the assessment of parenting it is stressed that a theoretical framework is essential to assessment. The authors comment bluntly that in contrast with their own clear theoretical framework, the problem with social work assessment based on the Orange Book, (Dept of Health, 1988), is that the latter 'contains an extensive list of recommended questions but provides no theoretical framework to help . . . make sense of the answers', (Reder and Lucey, 1995, p.5). They make no attempt to say what a social assessment theory should be but focus on attachment theory and intra-family interaction

61

as *their* theoretical framework. Compare also cognitive behavioural psychologists, whose approach to assessment is also strongly grounded in their claims for a competent theoretical framework, (McMurren and Hodge, 1994). These authors contend that it has been found that assessment programmes 'are more likely to be effective if they are explicitly based on a theoretical principle', (McMurren and Hodge, 1994, p.2). This is an important finding which applies generally across the social sciences. A recent paper on social work assessment agrees that the problem is that: 'there is no conceptual framework which adequately embraces the range of assessment tasks', (Lloyd and Taylor, 1995; cf. Boushel, 1994), and recent DOH research confirms the unacceptable deficiency of theory in assessments and case conferences, (Farmer and Owen, 1995, Ch.9).

Social workers do need a sound theoretical framework for assessment – one that can draw on intellectual foundations in the social sciences. The advantage of developing a methodology which is informed by a significant use of social science theory is not only in giving the use of various methods some consistency, and an improved degree of comparability, but also in giving social assessment the status it deserves, as an exacting and intellectually justifiable, as well as a skilful, procedure. Social workers need to be able to defend themselves not only on the basis of their assessments being based on research into specific risk and need factors, but also on the status of their method as being a distinctive kind of assessment – a social assessment – that is professional judgement informed by appropriate social research methodological principles.

However, there is an understandable scepticism in social and health work practice about the link between academic theory and professional élitism. The approach adopted here is one which takes into account the social and political context of practice and theory, attempting to draw on the practice wisdom of experienced social workers, as well as the theoretical contribution of the social sciences, *both* in the light of the critique of black and white feminist, disabled, and other anti-oppressive. In other words, it aims to offer a self-critical and reflexive account of assessment methods consistent with some current thinking in social research methodology, and open to the disagreement of workers, users' and user groups.

Foundations for critical auto/biographical methods
Assessment as a form of research
The problem for social work in the past has been that it has not been able to justify the kind of assessment it has needed to do. The understanding of individuals and families has drawn on psychological and psychiatric models, and there has been uncertainty as how to integrate these predominant models with

the social aspects of social work cases. However, in recent years there have been a number of developments in the area of social research methodology which now makes it possible to base social work assessment on a satisfactory theoretical framework, able to contextualise those of the psychologists or psychiatrists.

It is well known that qualitative social research into individual lives thrived briefly in the 1930s, but declined thereafter, but the situation now is very different. On the one hand there has been a flowering of qualitative research methodologies, often (but not exclusively) as a direct result of feminist work. Associated with this has been the revaluation of research into individual lives. So much so has this been true that there is now an enormous list of terms relating to it, emanating from various disciplines, including: interpretative biography; life history; oral narrative; case study; oral history; personal narrative; life stories; and auto/biography, (see Hatch and Wiesnewski, 1995, p.124 for others).

The practical implication of this is that the work of social assessment, which has often suffered from a problem of low status, can and should now be justified in terms of a *research* methodology, drawing on the variety of available models. It is rightly becoming a common theme in social- and health-related practice, that there is a close relationship between practice and research, and that practice can utilise, and justify, itself in terms of research methodology. In social work, Sheppard and others have called attention to this development, focusing on the parallels between the processes of research and practice, especially in the area of assessment (Everitt, 1992; Clifford and Cropper, 1995; Hart and Bond, 1995; Sheppard, 1995).

Sheppard uses a particular model of research method to show how qualitative research methodology should be applied in social assessments. In practice, this means that he focuses on three basic features: 1, the progressive and comparative development of clear hypotheses; 2, the search for disconfirming data; and 3, the reformulation of the hypothesis or redefinition of the problem in the face of disconfirming evidence. This enables workers to choose hypotheses which are least likely to be wrong, but depends on the practical application of routine scepticism about those hypotheses, and engagement in discussion about them, particularly with more-experienced workers, (thus drawing on a wider fund of practice wisdom). It appears to draw on assumptions which centre on the probability of truth, (Guba and Lincoln, 1994), but without accounting for values in sufficient depth. (see the debate between White, (1997) and Sheppard, (1998)).

The suggestion being made here is that a *Critical Auto/Biographical* framework provides a more defined and relevant methodology than Sheppard's outline of basic qualitative strategies. It highlights the fact that understanding the lives of others is closely connected to understanding the life of the assessor, and that both have to be critically contextualised by the presence of power and social difference. The concept is drawn from Liz Stanley's work, and the slash is designed to indicate the simultaneous inter-locking of biography and autobiography in the study of lives. It incorporates concepts drawn from different social science methodologies in a holistic, open-ended way that combines values and methodology, and is therefore primed for further development and criticism. The adjective 'critical' is intended to indicate the importance for present purposes of the link to perspectives which are critical of dominant assumptions, as indicated in the next section.

Integrating diverse perspectives
The need for powerful and subtle tools of analysis lies in the existence of major social divisions which involve fundamental differences of experience and perception (Clifford, 1994 and 1995). A consequence of this is that the question of values in social science is centre stage, because of the necessarily situated, participant status of any possible knower. It is therefore rational and desirable that values are themselves also the subject of discussion, and are openly and intentionally locked into a methodological framework, rather than cast in the role of hidden underpinning. The question of values is familiar territory in the social sciences, especially in contemporary debates about post-modernism, (cf. Squires, 1993), and the area of values is fundamental to basic principles for a methodology relevant to the applied social sciences. I have therefore tried to access the perspectives of people who are outside the dominant academic traditions. This is to make simultaneously an ethical and methodological choice – the need for which can be justified in sociological terms as an indispensable strategy for adequately understanding the social world in view of the dominance of established interests and concepts over our perception and creation of 'reality' (Scambler, 1996).

Basic principles can be found in the writings of women belonging to differing social divisions, who themselves have access to perspectives drawn from their own experience. For example, Patricia Hill Collins has attempted to elucidate basic principles of understanding in the social sciences, and deliberately not only drawn on her own experience as a black woman but has made a point of discussing her conclusions with other black women (Collins, 1990). This is seen not only as a matter of ethical practice, but reflects a theoretical position which can be derived from their discussion of social science method. There are a number of perspectives emanating from 'black feminisms', (the phrase itself is an over-simplification, (Nain, 1991; Mirza, 1997), but the contributions of people drawing on the experience of *other* oppressed groups also give access to those who are willing to listen to counterhegemonic perspectives (Personal Narratives Group, 1989). This means, for example, listening to the perspectives of disabled people who are not only critical of disabling physical environments (Oliver, 1992), but also critical of disabling social theories and methodologies (Oliver, 1992; Morris, 1992). I have also drawn on white feminists, including Lesbian writers, whose keen awareness of difference and reflexivity has been influential both in understanding the theory, and in the choice of terminology (Stanley, 1987; 1990; 1992; 1993; 1994; 1996; Stanley and Wise, 1983; 1994).

Summary of basic concepts

My understanding of these authors produces some basic principles, which overlap and have to be taken *together*. Each can be read differently depending on theory and interpretation. My aim here is not to argue for a closed (foundational or essentialist) system of concepts, but to contend that these principles can and should form the basis for a methodology of social assessment in health and social welfare simply because they provide the best account currently available of how to understand and position oneself as a participant and observer in making a social assessment. The key principles of this framework can be summarised as follows:

1. Methodology and Oppression

It is essential that the methods used to understand and assess people and social situations are self-critically linked to a relevant research methodology in relation to their content, form, process, and procedure, and that this methodology is informed by the perspectives of oppressed groups them-selves. There is therefore an explicit value-slope built into this framework, exemplified in the way *critical auto/biography* draws upon the perspectives of different oppressed groups.

2. Social Difference

It is important to systematically analyse social differences that exist between the dominant and dominated social groups of all the major social divisions within society, usually identified as 'race', class, gender, sexual preference, disability, and age. Differences can also be identified in relation to other social divisions, e.g. health status, religion, region. Differences within and across the social divisions categories also have to be thoroughly taken into account. The complexity of oppression arises from their complex changing social construction – their interconnections and overlaps, specific to particular circumstances, times, places, individuals, and groups.

3. Reflexivity

The assessor has to be understood as a participant within the theoretical and practical framework. The mutual involvement of the observer and the observed implies that their perceptions interact. The *values* and perspectives of both are therefore central to the process of assessment. However, this process can only be understood in the context of the power differentials between them. This personal interaction is thus understood not only in psychological terms but also as a matter of sociology, history, ethics, and politics.

4. Historical Location in Time and Space

Rather than basing social histories on psychological developmental theories, life experiences and events need to be related to concrete times and places in the process of constructing historical and sociological accounts of their changing lives. Multidisciplinary connections should be sought between individual, family, community, and social histories, including their medical and psychological histories, which are thus given a real, concrete, geographical, and historical context, focusing on the specific, rather than using general categories of either psychological or sociological analysis.

5. Interacting Social Systems

The individual's situation should be viewed in relation to various interacting social systems. This includes the family, peer groups, organisations, communities, and so on up to and including the international context. However, unlike some traditional systems approaches it is *not* assumed that these systems function homoestatically (they do not always adjust themselves successfully when disturbed by internal or external changes), nor that they are autonomous, nor that their identification is incontestable, nor that system functions necessarily override human agency. This means that causation may be internal or external to a system, and that the definition and continued functioning of a system cannot be assumed but should be assessed within changing historical circumstances.

6. Power

Power issues in social relationships need to be examined at multiple levels: at the level of political, social, and economic structures, *and* at the level of personal power arising from cultural, institutional, and psychological factors. Power may be exercised over people tacitly or overtly, but may also be actively produced and wielded by people, and may be used positively or negatively. The bottom line of analysis is the access of individuals, groups, and agencies to physical and material resources. It is essential to analyse the distribution of material wealth and power, including the simultaneous impact of unequal power relationships in the present, and the historical accumulation of cultural and economic capital against which oppressed groups struggle.

Although this framework of principles has been deliberately drawn from writers with anti-oppressive political and ethical commitments, it can readily be seen that it connects with many contemporary and traditional themes in the philosophy of the social sciences, in multi-disciplinary approaches to life history research, and also in post-modern, post-structuralist thought. The theoretical aspects of this framework are further discussed in Part One of *Social Assessment Theory and Practice* (Clifford, 1998). The framework thus represents the best in the traditions of social work practice yet can draw on the latest paradigms of social research, its sensitivity to varying perspectives and values having always been a part of social work concerns about making professional judgements in complex situations.

Practice
The above framework has not simply been deduced from theoretical considerations but has been researched and tested in co-operation with experienced social workers and trainers. Indeed it has been drawn (inevitably) partly from the experience of social work practice of the writer, and especially from the experience of observing and working with black, white, and Lesbian women colleagues and service users. The framework has emerged over a number of years, and one source of information has been research conducted into assessment methods in fostering and adoption, which has already been reported (Clifford and Cropper, 1994; 1997a; 1997b; Clifford, 1999). However, more recently there has been the development of joint training and research with a social services department, in which this conceptual framework was used as a unifying basis for developing a course concerned with updating and improving the assessment of needs and risks in initial and comprehensive assessments in child and family care. It was also used to investigate and discuss with experienced childcare workers how they have been assessing children prior to the course, and how their understanding of their work has been supported and interrogated as a result of experiencing the course. It has now been run three times with the approval of senior management, and is presented with the active involvement of both academic staff and departmental staff from social services. It has required considerable liaison and development of trust, but the

outcomes have been very worth while in view of the positive response from social workers under great pressure of work, many of whom having considerable experience of assessment of difficult family situations involving all the various forms of child abuse and distress.

The training/research was planned jointly, and involved input from a senior social worker, as well as the child protection co-ordinator and training officer. The plan agreed was for four separate days of training, two to be devoted to understanding basic methodological issues involved in social work assessment, including multidisciplinary and multiprofessional issues, theory, and values. The following two days would be centred on the narrower issues of using specific forms of assessment in child care in the critical light of a grasp of the methodology, focusing particularly on needs assessments and risks assessments in varying circumstances. This would include looking at alternative approaches to these kinds of assessments, based on differing disciplinary and differing professional contexts. The aim would be to actively use the strengths of existing practices, involving practitioners in a dialogue, but offering supportive materials to develop further their assessment methods in the light of current developments in both academic and social services contexts. The following gives a very brief outline of the event (the details have been omitted and have in any case changed as the course has developed).

Learning Objectives
1.   To understand basic methodological principles and values involved in social assessment.
2.   To be able to apply principles in theory and practice using and interpreting information and a variety of pro formas and schedules for assessment.
3.   To rethink practice implications for assessment and intervention.

Methods
1.   Presentation of policy and theoretical frameworks – specifically the methodological principles for social assessment.
2.   Using computer software case material to illustrate theoretical principles.
3.   Using and interpreting CCIS computer-based research evidence in relation to case material.
4.   Presentation of an array of pro formas and schedules for assessment of abuse and neglect.

5. Small peer group discussion of schedules in relation to own case material and the theoretical framework.
6. Assessment, planning, intervention, and court work.

As a result of this initiative the department concerned has been sufficiently encouraged by the reactions of social workers to commit itself to the training of all child care workers using this model. There are numerous possible reasons for this development, including inspection of local authority standards of assessment in child care, and the need to be seen to be taking action, especially in the light of past failures. However, one of the reasons for the favourable reception of the framework is its compatibility with the traditions of good social work practice, which has often been more subtle than is sometimes appreciated. This compatibility is evidenced in social workers' evaluation of it as supportive of their efforts.

The critical auto/biographical concepts that underpin this theoretical framework for social assessment are thus not presented as radically new departures from established practice, but (critically) support and develop existing traditions within the profession. They offer the chance of reskilling workers in methods which make sense to them because of both their past training and education and their commitment to values which have (unevenly) reflected women's experiences of care and caring. Awareness in the best practitioners of concepts such as social difference, interacting social systems, reflexivity, power, and historical location is not something that struck them as foreign when they began to reflect on how they were actually assessing their own cases. On the contrary, we found it constantly emerging in their discussion of detailed cases. As one course member noted: 'A lot of these issues are unconsciously considered in practice but it's good to refresh your understanding of why these things are important, and can help to put a situation in context.' When presented with the conceptual framework there was (after some mutual adjustment of language and form) wide recognition that this *was* a reflection of their thinking which simultaneously supported and challenged them – and they expressed satisfaction and interest in having an intellectual basis for their work. Yet they also conceded that the theoretical framework made them review and think harder about the cases in which they were currently involved: '. . . it enabled me to question and enhance my knowledge base'.

Practitioners could appreciate the relationship between the theoretical framework and more-specific assessment guidelines and schedules with its implications of uncertainty and process, requiring professional judgement.

They appreciated the reflexive element in the framework which supports the central role of judgement and evaluation. They were able to use the key principles not only to inform and question their own particular judgements but also as a means of questioning the schedules and pro formas which were presented to them. These included old standards with which they were familiar such as the 'Orange Book' but a range of old and new local and national frameworks for assessment in all sorts of situations, drawing on differing disciplines and forms of expertise. Social work has traditionally drawn on a range of methods for assessment (Milner and O'Byrne, 1998), and this needs to be seen as a strength rather than a weakness. In terms of the post-modernist emphasis on anti-foundationalism and diversity 'social work method' can be said to be in advance of current thinking rather than behind it – precisely because of its longstanding awareness of diversity of perspectives, and its willingness to embrace multidisciplinary concepts. The theoretical framework presented here does nothing to decrease this respect for diversity, but it does provide an intellectual 'home' – an awareness of the approximate centre of gravity of a *social* work assessment and the means to critique and evaluate other approaches. Practitioners demonstrated during the course that they were confident to critique the various schedules and methods of assessment proposed using these concepts.

The course has now run three times, involving nearly 50 experienced social workers from differing child care settings, and the response throughout has been overwhelmingly positive, the more so as we improved our presentation. In its most recent version only one of the participants did not give the course the maximum score on a rating scale, and the sole exception was because of the 'need for more time to digest information and reflect' – an objection with which we could readily sympathise. A common reaction was that the framework and information presented made workers 'much more confident' about their own practice. The combined effect of low social position in relation to other professionals and the apparent *absence* of a theoretical framework often means that neither the social assessment nor the social worker gets the respect deserved. Course participants were keenly aware of this from their own experience and responded to something which though theoretical had relevance to a vital area of practice. This applies, of course, not only to childcare social workers: other areas of social assessment including mental health and community care are discussed in relation to this theoretical framework elsewhere (Clifford, 1998, Part Two). The recent developments in social research methodology, especially feminist contributions, and the perspectives of oppressed groups which are welded together in the critical auto/biographical framework make it possible to envisage social work moving forward more confidently. There will never be an end to making disputable and difficult judgements about human social situations, but at least the profession can move forward knowing that there *is* an eminently arguable case for what social workers have been trying to do and a guiding framework of concepts for critically evaluating progress and developing further.

The framework justifies (up to a point) some of the traditional approaches to social work assessment, but brings it in line with contemporary social theory and values. It provides a basis for 'making a difference' as a recognised profession with a similar standing to other professions. This is one of the longstanding aims of the profession for which the Chair of BASW has again called (Conway, 1999). The proposed General Social Care Council may prescribe standards of conduct but without a theoretical framework upon which to base assessment, the intellectual validity of social assessment in relation to other forms of assessment will not be recognised and social workers will remain devalued. The value and effectiveness of partnership with other professions will be undermined without confidence in one's own position. This methodology helps to provide the 'absent framework' that is required but in a self-critical way that recognises the inevitability and significance of partial, located judgements made in situations of 'partnership' with both service users and other professions.

References

Boushel, M (1995) 'Keeping safe: strengthening the protective environment of children in foster care' *Adoption and Fostering* 18(1), pp 33-9

Clifford, D J (1992/3) 'Towards an anti-oppressive social work assessment method' *Practice*, 6(3), pp 60-9

Clifford, D J (1994) 'Critical life histories: a key anti-oppressive research method', in Humphries, B and Trueman, C (eds) *Rethinking Social Research* London, Avebury, pp 102-22

Clifford, D J (1995) 'Methods in oral history and social work' *Oral History* 24(2), pp 65-70

Clifford, D J (1996) 'Biography and social assessment in health and social services' (unpublished paper presented to The Centre for Ageing and Biographical Studies at the Open University and The Centre for Policy on Ageing, London, 21 June)

Clifford, D J (1998) *Social Assessment Theory and Practice: A Multi-Disciplinary Framework* Aldershot, Hants, Ashgate

Clifford, D J (1999) Developing a Research Methodology for Social Work Assessment in Adoption and Fostering, in British Agencies for Adoption and Fostering *Assessment, Preparation and Support: Implications from Research* London, BAAF, pp 47-57

Clifford, D J and Cropper, A (1994) 'Applying auto/biography: researching the assessment of life experiences' *Auto/Biography* 3(1) and 3(2), (Double Issue), pp 47-58

Clifford, D J and Cropper, A (1997a) 'Individual assessment of potential carers: essential methods' *Practice* 9(1), pp 47-59

Clifford, D J and Cropper, A (1997b) 'Parallel processes in researching and assessing potential carers' *Child and Family Social Work* 2(4), pp 235-46

Collins, PH (1990) *Black Feminism* London, Unwin

Conway, L (1999) 'Social workers can revitalise a tired society' *Professional Social Work* Birmingham, BASW, April Issue, p 4

Cropper, A (1995) Applying a Black Feminist approach to Social Work Assessment (unpublished M.Phil Dissertation), Liverpool, Liverpool John Moores University

Cropper, A (1997) 'Rethinking Practice: Learning from a Black Feminist Perspective' in Bates, J, Pugh, R and Thompson, N (eds) *Protecting Children: Challenges and Changes* Aldershot, Arena, pp 31-41

Department of Health (1988) *Protecting Children: A Guide for Social Workers Undertaking a Comprehensive Assessment* London: HMSO

Everitt, A *et al.*, (1992) *Applied Research for Better Practice* London, Macmillan

Farmer, E and Owen, M (1995) *Child Protection Practice: Private Risks and Public Remedies* London, HMSO

Guba, E G and Lincoln, Y S (1994) 'Competing paradigms in qualitative research' in Denzin, N Kand Lincoln, Y S (eds) *Handbook of Qualitative Research* London, Sage, pp 105-17

Hart, E and Bond, M (1995) *Action Research for Health and Social Care* Milton Keynes, Open University Press

Hatch, J A and Wiesnewsky, R (eds) (1995) *Life History and Narrative* London, Falmer Press

Lloyd, M and Taylor, C (1995) 'From Hollis to the Orange Book: developing a holistic model of social work assessment in the 1990s' *British Journal of Social Work* 25(6), pp 691-710

McMurren, M and Hodge, J (1994), *The Assessment of Criminal Behaviours of Clients in Secure Settings* London, Jessica Kingsley

Milner, J and O'Byrne, P (1998) *Assessment in Social Work* London, MacMillan

Mirza, H S (ed.) (1997) *Black British Feminism* London, Routledge

Morris, J (1992) 'Personal and political: a feminist perspective on researching physical disability' *Disability, Handicap and Society* 7(2), pp 110-21

Nain, G T (1991) 'Black or Anti-racist feminism?' *Feminist Review* 37, pp 63-74

Personal Narratives Group, (1989) *Interpreting Women's Lives* Bloomington: Indiana University Press

Reder, P, Duncan, S, Gray, M (1993) *Beyond Blame: Child Abuse Tragedies Revisited* London, Routledge

Reder, P and Lucey C (eds) (1995) *Assessment of Parenting: Psychiatric and Psychological Contributions* London, Routledge

Scambler, G (1996) 'The "project of modernity" and the parameters for a critical sociology: an argument with illustrations from sociology' *Sociology* 30(3), pp 567-81

Sheppard, M (1995) 'Social work, social science and practice wisdom', British Journal of Social Work, 25, pp 265-293

Sheppard, M (1998), 'Practice validity, reflexivity and knowledge for social work' *British Journal of Social Work* 28, pp

Squires, J (ed.) (1993) *Principled Positions: Postmodernism and the Rediscovery of Values* London: Lawrence and Wishart

Stanley, L (ed.) (1990) *Feminist Praxis* London: Routledge

Stanley, L (1992) *The Auto/Biographical I: The Theory and Practice of Feminist Auto/biography* Manchester: Manchester University Press

Stanley, L and Wise, S (1983) *Breaking Out: Feminist Consciousness and Feminist Research* London, Routledge

Stanley, L and Wise, S (1994) *Breaking Out Again: Feminist Ontology and Epistemology* Manchester, Manchester University Press

White, S (1997) 'Beyond retroduction? Hermeneutics, reflexivity and social work practice' *British Journal of Social Work* 23, pp739–54

Chapter 7
Action for Inclusion: Social work – making a difference with refugee children.
Cathy Aymer and Toyin Okitikpi

Introduction

Much of the literature on migration has been concerned with the ways in which society has adapted to accommodate immigrants. Over the last 50 years the wave of migration to Britain has changed dramatically. For example in the first half of the 1900s continental Europe provided the main scene of refugee flow as people moved from country to country trying to avoid war or the aftermath of war. Organised refugee relief was considered a 'European phenomenon' (Ruthstrom-Ruin 1993). From the 1960s towards the close of the 1990s the vast majority of refugees into Britain were people from Africa and southern Asia. The pattern has shifted again since the collapse of communism in eastern and central Europe and as a result of the wars in the Balkans more people from these regions are seeking refugee status and asylum in Britain. What is evident however is that, in more recent years a European-wide clampdown on migrants, especially those from Africa and Asia, has led to a greater use of detention centres at the port of entry.

The public is aware that regimes in some of these countries are brutal and oppressive against, not just people who try to oppose them, but also whole sections of society. For example, individuals are as likely to face oppression and persecution as members of social or ethnic groups who are considered to be against the interests of the ruling government. It is not surprising that those who fall within these categories would try to escape persecution by fleeing to Britain, which is still perceived as a haven, a place of refuge where they can live in relative safety. They seek political asylum, but are often faced with an immigration system that is both unyielding and discriminatory. In addition to the structural obstacles there are also negative attitudes with which the refugees have to contend. These attitudes come from the popular perception that these are really economic refugees, who see Britain as a land of opportunity and possibilities. It is believed that they are choosing Britain because of the 'generous' and freely available social welfare system and because, compared with other European countries, it is still considered much easier to enter.

Whilst this vexed wrangling of whether they are bona fide asylum seekers goes on, what is often forgotten is that a large number of these refugees are children, many of which have been rescued or forced to flee some of the most damaging and brutal social environments in order to get to relative safety. In many cases the children may have travelled long distances, passing through a third or fourth country before finally arriving in Britain. In essence it is the experiences of this group of children as they come into contact with the social services and the education system that we wish to study.

- These are the broad range of questions that the research study aimed to investigate and analyse.

- What happens to these children once they arrive?

- How do social services departments and education departments respond to them?

- What are the criteria that are used to determine whether any of these children would be offered services as a result of the trauma they may have experienced?

- What form does this help take?

The international context

The plight of refugees and asylum seekers continues to be the most tragic development of the twentieth century. Millions of people are on the move throughout the world, fleeing famine, persecution, oppression, and war. It is estimated that there are some 19 million people who are refugees worldwide, and in relation to the three African countries that are the subject of this research study, Hitchcox (1990) observed:

> *In Sudan, Somalia and Ethiopia, the problems of civil war and invasion have been worsened by devastating famines and drought. These countries host each other's refugees; by 1988 there were 800,000 Ethiopian refugees in Somalia who had fled there in search of safety and food. At the same time, Ethiopia was giving asylum to 500,000 Somalia refugees* (Hitchcox 1990:11) .

By 1995 the figures had changed to well over 600,000 Somali refugees and 400,000 Sudanese who are refugees and another 4,000,000 who are internally displaced people (IDP); the figures for Ethiopia were estimated as over 1,300,000 Ethiopian and Eritrean refugees in Somalia and Sudan and that at least 2,000,000 other people have been forced to leave their homes in Ethiopia.

As Ruthstrom-Ruin (1993) observed, the problem of displaced people, asylum seekers, and refugees has a long history and as a form of recognition of this phenomenon the 1951 UN Convention and the 1967 UN Protocol defined refugees and those with refugee status as those who 'owing to a well founded fear of being persecuted for reasons of race, religion, nationality, membership of a particular social group or political opinion' have had to flee their homes. Asylum seekers are defined as people who have had to flee their homes and cross an internationally recognised border in search of a place of refuge, a place of safety.

Both the 1951 UN Convention and the 1967 UN Protocol were deemed to be inadequate and too narrow in their definition and, as Rutter (1994) highlighted, the Organisation of African Unity (OAU) broadened the definition of refugees to take into account people who are compelled to leave their homes and country of origin by external aggressors or domination from without. Their definition also includes those who have had to flee as a result of what are termed as events that seriously undermine public order. The experience of the Chinese population in Indonesia, Tutsis in Rwanda, Eritreans in Ethiopia, and the Sudanese Christians in Sudan are perhaps the best example of the group that the OAU's definition embraces.

In essence the OAU's definition is more inclusive and encompassing, taking account of the complex nature of social relations, social developments, and ethnic rivalry and conflicts that exist within and between countries. This definition acknowledged that for many people threats to their lives could come from both within and without. The OAU's approach is an attempt to provide a more realistic definition of what actually happens to people who are caught in a social environment that threatens their very existence. As well as the dramatic scenes of full-scale war, many of the children and families seeking asylum and refugee status are victims of low intensive physical and psychological warfare, or they may be subject to inter-ethnic and religious persecution (Rutter 1994). Having fled persecution, torture, and abuse into the safety of another country there are no guarantees that this will bring about peace and tranquillity to their lives. In many cases some children and their families are exposed to the harsh reality of living in temporary camps and transitional accommodation that are as dangerous, frightening, and life threatening as the places they have fled.

The British experience
In Britain the number of refugees is estimated to have increased substantially since the mid-1980s. It is suggested that most cities in Britain are now home to many refugees from different parts of the world. According to a Methodist Church publication, in 1994 it was estimated that there were 22,500 refugee pupils between the ages of 5 and 16 years attending London schools, with

another 2,000 outside London. In 1995 the number had risen to 27,000. The Church's report also mentioned that, of the asylum seekers and refugees in the UK, 'it is only a minority who have their families with them. Most have had to flee very quickly and have not been able to arrange for their families to leave as well' (Methodist Resource 1996:4).

For many children and their families the experience of being a refugee and asylum seeker is both physically and emotionally shattering whilst for some children the implication of being an unaccompanied refugee is immense. Not only could they have lost contact with their families but they also find themselves in a strange country, where the people are very different, where the language is perhaps incomprehensible and different and they are in an alien social and cultural environment that is in many cases unwelcoming.

A child's eye view
It is possible to suggest that children caught up in a destabilising social environment where they have had to flee their home and be placed in transitory or short-to medium-term accommodation may experience both emotional and psychological uncertainties. For many of them the feelings of uncertainty and instability are often further compounded by the traumatic events they have witnessed. However, the term 'trauma' is but a shorthand description of unimaginable events and experiences that are beyond comprehension. What is evident from our research into the experiences of children from Somalia, Sudan, and Ethiopia is that many of them have had experiences that continue to cause them pain and anxiety. The sheer scale of the dangers and difficulties many of the children had to endure was illustrated by Warner (1996), who wrote:

> *In 1988 thousands of children started to trek across Southern Sudan seeking refuge from the fighting. Most of these unaccompanied children were boys aged between seven and seventeen. Some had been separated from their families in the confusion of the fighting. In fleeing many of the boys thought the journey to Ethiopia would take a few days; in fact it took six to ten weeks. Some of the children were killed or died of hunger and exhaustion. . . . . By 1991 there were about 17,000 unaccompanied Sudanese refugee children in the camps of Ethiopia. In May 1991 following the overthrow of government the Sudanese refugees were forced to flee back to Sudan, through heavy rain, while being bombed (Warner 1996:41).*

There is a sense that many of the children are having to hold onto an integrated self amidst what must appear to them as a fragmented, incoherent, violent, and brutal adult world. What is further evident from our research and supported by previous documented evidence (Athey 1991, Burgess 1992,

Herman 1992) is the devastation caused to the inner world of many of the children as a result of what Erikson (1994) described as 'acute or accumulative negative experiences'. It is acknowledged that children have a different way of seeing the world compared with adults, they view the world not necessarily from a naïve and innocent standpoint but from the eye view of those who are untainted by ironies and conventions. What is evident is that children do not rationalise the world in the same ways as their parents. They do not understand why they have had to leave their home and move into another country, where, in their view, the situation seems much worse. For some, although they may have witnessed horrific events and be very frightened, scarred and emotionally and psychologically damaged by what they have experienced, they may also feel a similar depth of despair about the home they can no longer go to, the friends, relatives, and neighbours they could no longer see, their own school which they can no longer attend, or about their precious possessions which are forever lost to them.

Impact of trauma on the children
The events that many children from Sudan, Somalia, and Ethiopia have witnessed and endured have had a profound effect on their lives and in the way many of the children relate to people around them. It is now widely accepted that many refugee children suffer from traumatisation and uprootedness. Though originally a surgical concept, trauma 'has become a useful metaphor for characterising the breaking point in the lives of people who continue to suffer from repetitive death fears and of severe constriction of the personality'(Dasberg *et al.*,1987:1). Defined in various ways, what is common in the definitions is that it describes 'any experience that causes the child unbearable pain' (Kalsched 1996:1) or, as Kohut (1977:104) suggests, trauma is best described as 'an unnameable dread associated with the threatening dissolution of a coherent self'. Similarly but with more emphasis on the psychological and the physicality of the experience Erikson (1994:223) takes trauma to mean 'a blow to the psyche that breaks through one's defences so sudden and with such brutal force that one cannot react on it effectively'

Focusing much more on the wider social and environmental consideration, uprooting is described as

> *'the experience of being forced to leave one's familiar surroundings and to settle in a new and unfamiliar environment for an indefinite period, which brings stress and can cause various long-lasting adjustment problems. Often the fear of being expelled causes paralysis; also feelings of helplessness, sadness, anger as well as aggressive and self-destructive impulses. These feelings and impulses interfere with efforts to adapt to the new environment, such as learning the language or building up a social network.'* (Van der Veer 1998:23.)

Here and now

It is understandable that local authority workers and other welfare agency workers should concentrate all their efforts on trying to ensure that the children (accompanied and unaccompanied) are given the necessary services and provision to which they are entitled. In the first instance the focus is often on ensuring that accommodation is located, the appropriate financial support is provided, and the children and their family's legal status, if accompanied, is given special attention to alleviate the anxieties of being deported, perhaps back to where they have just escaped. Additionally, for children of school age, the workers have to work with the education departments with the view to getting them placed in schools that are able to accommodate them.

Rightly, the practical problems that have been identified by the workers need to be urgently addressed, as they require quick responses, so that it is possible to begin to look towards the long-term needs of the children. However, evidence from this research suggests that, because of the problem-focused nature of the approach, and the emphasis on practical matters, there seems to be little time given to reflecting on the experiences of these children. In essence, welfare workers and teachers are more confident about working with practical aspects of the children's needs but they are less certain as to how far to probe into their lives or to encourage them to talk about their experiences in an informal way.

For many of these children arrival in Britain is not only the end of their journey but it is also, perhaps, the beginning of a much longer journey because sandwiched between fleeing their home and country and arriving in Britain are the traumatic events that they have had to endure. These events and their experience of them could come to symbolise the defining moment in their lives. They could inevitably play a major role in the development of their future and cannot and should not be underplayed nor should their impact on the lives of the children be minimised. In many cases the events are psychologically, physically, and emotionally transforming and for some children the experiences are so profound that they might dislocate them from the world around them.

Although trauma, and in particular childhood trauma, has been 'a social issue and problem throughout civilisation' (Burgess 1992:xiii) it is only in the last 20 years that work on trauma has seriously begun to look at the experiences of children. Much of the impetus came from child abuse work but increasingly more attention is being paid to children from countries where there are high- and low-intensity wars as well as children whose experiences result from naturally occurring and unpredictable disasters.

Attempting to make a difference

The way that welfare professionals and their agencies respond to these children is fragmented and idiosyncratic. This lack of consistency, even at the basic level, has meant that many children are provided with minimum support and there appears to be less attention being paid to their long-term well-being. In our analysis of the responses from the statutory and voluntary organisations that we researched we found that children, especially those who are 'unaccompanied', may be referred by immigration to the local authority SSDs at the port of arrival. Once the social work duty team receives the referral, either directly from the airport or seaport, there is then what can only be described as a crisis management approach to working with the children. For example, evidence suggests that in practice the immediate crisis of providing shelter for the children is dealt with very well. Whether other issues that the children may be presenting are considered and whether a full 'assessment' takes place depend on individual social workers. In most cases we discovered that a comprehensive service that takes account of the needs of the children is dependent on whether there is a worker within the office who is interested in this area.

There is great room for 'discretion'. Part of the difficulty is that whilst there are Department of Health guidelines on working with refugee children and asylum seekers, our research found that in most instances the local authority social services department may or may not have a set of written procedures concerning these children.

There is also an issue about how local authorities should respond to the plight of such children and whether they should become involved in refugee and asylum claims. For many authorities over-stretched resources and lack of additional practical support from central government have meant they have had to meet, fully or partially, the financial burden of providing for these children.

By way of explanation some authorities asserted that, aside from the resources issues, there are additional difficulties and conflicts that arise over roles between the competing agencies. In their view many of the problems stem from the overlap of duties, responsibilities, and roles and until these are dealt with it is likely that the poor level of response to the children will continue.

On the other hand voluntary organisations such as the Refugee Council may become involved through a referral from the Home Office or again directly from immigration. They will assist with asylum claims and arrange legal advice for children and families. There is a special Children's Panel that deals with unaccompanied children. This organisation may also refer on to local authorities to deal with ongoing care. They claim to experience great differences in response from different London boroughs and claim that some individual social workers are far more willing to become involved than others. They also witness many arguments between authorities about who is responsible for particular children. Their involvement is really on a crisis basis and they do not provide ongoing therapy or support.

In a different but more involved way the voluntary organisations like the Medical Foundation do provide ongoing specialist support and therapy for children and families. However, they are a small organisation and, it seems, only become involved when there is a crisis or 'problem'. Overall, then, there does not seem to be much evidence of a coordinated or multidisciplinary approach to providing care or support for these children. There is also the potential for great variation between individual authorities and even between individual area offices.

Joined up approach
Increasingly, it is acknowledged that at the macro level it is important for the UN and national governments to take an interdisciplinary approach to the work with refugees and asylum seekers. Too often governments have made decisions which in the shortterm have served their national interest but in the longterm have hindered efforts to bring about workable and sustainable solutions. Similarly the evidence from this research is that whilst there are indications that some local authority social services and education departments are trying to provide adequate services and support for refugee children who have experienced trauma, the approach taken is akin to the short-termism described above. In many cases evidence points to social services departments uncertain as to how to approach their work with this group of children. They seem understandably reluctant about getting involved and perhaps getting in too deep with the children and their families.

Conclusion
This research into the experience of traumatised refugee children is still in progress and what is evident from the data so far is that many local authorities, both education and social services, and voluntary organisations are striving and working very hard to provide services for refugee children who are located within their sphere of duty and responsibility. In many cases help and support are provided despite the inadequate level of resources that has been made available to them by central government. What is also evident is that local authorities in particular are not operating from a politically neutral position. In most cases they are having to weigh whether to concentrate their limited resources on servicing their ongoing commitments to their constituents against

the humanitarian considerations of providing basic requirements for children and their families who have fled oppressive regimes, famine, or war. As well as internal financial and resources pressures local authorities also face those externally from council tax payers and a hostile tabloid press who accuse them of ignoring denizens whilst providing luxury accommodation and unwarranted financial support for refugee families and bogus asylum seekers.

One possible, revolutionary solution could be to remove the duties and responsibilities of providing for refugees and asylum seekers from local authorities and place them in the hands of a much expanded and adequately funded refugee council. They would then be given full powers to negotiate to lease properties from housing departments, have places available in schools with additional support for the children, and the purchase of services from social services. However, since this is an unlikely possibility a more comprehensive approach, similar to the child protection process, needs to be considered for children. Even with a qualifying statement that there are exceptions to the rule, the case for the impact of early childhood experiences on adult life has already been made. We believe that social services and the education departments need to look more closely at their approaches to working with this group of children.

There is evidence that because of the turbulence in world affairs, where internal ethnic strife, religious intolerance, racism, calls for independence, and the impact of globalisation are all making their presence felt, the problems of refugees and asylum seekers are more likely to increase rather than decrease.

It is imperative that social workers have an understanding of the ongoing nature of the problem because it is they who are charged with the responsibility of considering 'what is in the best interest of children'. It is necessary to ensure that the children are appropriately assessed and the necessary services provided, because failure to identify the children's problems early or address their needs, even within the limitations of the resources constraints, means that many of them are likely to join the ranks of the excluded which, in the long term, would be more costly, both to local authorities and central government. As Rystad 1990, rightly observed:

> *The refugee problem is as multifaceted and complex as it is immense. No single research project can deal with it in its entirety, but only hope to make a contribution by focusing on a limited part, a specific perspective or a certain aspect of the problem.* (Rystad 1990:7.)

References
Athey, J (1991) *Refugee Children, Theory, Research and Services* Baltimore, John Hopkins University Press

Burgess, A W(ed.) (1992) *Child Trauma: Issues and research* USA Garland

Butler, I and Williams, H (1994) *Children Speak: Children, Trauma and Social Work* London, NSPCC and Longman

Dasberg, H, Davidson, S *et al.*, (1987) *Society and Trauma of War* Van Gorcum

Erikson, K (1994) *New Species of Trouble Exploration in Disaster, Trauma and Community* USA, W W Norton & Co

Herman, J L (1992) *Trauma and Recovery from Domestic Abuse to Political Terror* London, Pandora

Hithcox, L (1990) *Refugees* London, Franklin Watts

Johnson, K (1989) *Trauma in the Lives of Children* London, Macmillan

Kelsched, D (1996) T*he Inner World of Trauma: Archetypal Defences of the Personal Spirit* London, Routledge

Kohut, H (1977) *The Restoration of Self* New York, International Universities Press

Methodist Resources (1996) *Refugee Children. Children of War* London, Betty Press

Ruthstrom-Ruin, C (1993) *Beyond Europe: The Globalisation of Refugee Aid* Berlin, Lund University Press

Rutter, J (1994) *Refugee Children in the Classroom* London, Trentham Books

Rystad, G (1990) *The uprooted. Forced Migration as an International Problem in the Cold War Era* Berlin, Lund University Press

Van der Veer, G (1998) *Counselling and therapy with Refugees and victims of Trauma* (second edition) USA, Wiley

Warner, R (1996) *Refugees: Global issues* USA, Wayland

Chapter 8
Disability, Dependency and the Role of the Professional
Jennifer Harris and John Stewart

Introduction

In this chapter we shall discuss the nature of the relationship which disabled people have with the Welfare State. Rights to services and benefits have been just one of the tactics which the modern disability movement has used in its overall strategy to achieve the inclusion of disabled people in mainstream society. In the area of income maintenance, it was relatively easy to attach their cause to that of the general pressure for legally enforceable rights to social security. The pursuit of welfare rights for disabled people was entirely justified on grounds of equality. It would have been impossible for disabled people to even begin to consider themselves as part of mainstream economic and social life without very specific rights. As Oliver has explained, the Union of Physically Impaired Against Segregation sought the 'necessary financial . . . and other help required from the state to enable us to gain the maximum possible independence in daily living activities, to achieve mobility, undertake productive work and to live where and how we choose with full control over our lives' (cited in Oliver, 1996: 24).

Extending welfare rights as part of this general struggle has proved difficult enough; however, even when achieved, exercising those rights was made to seem problematic in two ways. First the neo-classical liberal critique of the Welfare State under Thatcherite regimes portrayed receipt of social security as the main part of dependency culture – disabled people became part of the 'underclass' for which the New Labour euphemism is the 'socially excluded'. The second problem lies in disabled people having to trade their 'deserving' privileged and quasi-charitable status for rights and entitlements. The idea of a right to a privilege is just feudal. Disabled people must now compete on more or less the same terms with all the other groups who seek more-equitable treatment over income maintenance. Housing is a useful example of the tensions and contradictions which exist in our Welfare State between a rights and a needs approach to entitlement to benefits and services because paying for social rented housing involves claiming a social security benefit, but obtaining a tenancy in the first instance is determined by the establishment of housing needs by an expert (that is, not the applicant). The circularity of this argument is completed when we realise that in struggling for acceptance of their claim to have rights to benefits and services, disabled people become enmeshed in a dependency relationship with the Welfare State.

The foundations of welfare for disabled people

In the late 1970s, it was at last recognised that social services could be neither benevolent nor disinterested over their administration of welfare. It was also recognised that the 'social problem' focus of traditional social administration had been as ideologically constructed as any other stance. Thus, all the welfare provisions, from the reforming times of the post-war Labour government down to the 1970s, needed to be critically reappraised. Questions were raised such as: whose perception of the needs of disabled people was being served by the extant welfare services?; were the needs of the former group of paramount importance and what was the role of the 'expert' in determining needs?

The Act, which set the foundation stone, is in fact very thin on provisions (National Assistance Act 1948, sec. 29). With regard to welfare, that Act did most of its job in Section 1 by abolishing the Poor Laws! Having put no serious critical thought into what new 'welfare arrangements for blind, deaf, dumb and crippled persons' might be about, social administrators simply conveyed the medical model of disability which had served under the Poor Laws and assumed 'experts' would deal with the intricacies of practice in relation to disabled people. Their proposed 'solutions' primarily focused upon the amelioration of the more obvious effects of 'impairment' by the provision of aids and adaptations and by providing institutions.

However, critics were beginning to ask what was the purpose of various welfare measures; whose purposes were being served by them? The service providers of the Welfare State began to be characterised as agents of social control, dependency, and patriarchy. It is not too far-fetched to suppose that if social administration had not radically reinvented itself it would just have been swept aside by the powerfully explanatory and burgeoning critiques of which feminism is probably the leader, but of which the social model of disability is certainly another. These new social movements had both explanatory force and a commitment to welfare very different from the patrician order of traditional social administration.

The 16 sections of Part III of the National Assistance Act 1948, which were supposed to be the foundation of provision for disabled people in the post-war Welfare State were ambivalent in focus since they also sought to control the extent to which the State should accept responsibility for either the satisfaction of needs or the amelioration of problems arising from impairment. Thus, from the outset both medical model and social model issues arose, although it is clear with hindsight that only the former were acted upon in the resultant provisions. The nature of the institutional provision along with the determination of

Parliament to ensure that the needs of disabled people were defined by local authorities, represented a clear continuation of the Poor Law, and even subsequent legislation, down to the NHS and Community Care Act 1990 reinforced this position. Titmuss wrote of this:

> *General agreement was reached in Britain during the 1940s that the poor law should be abolished; the philosophy by which it was upheld and the means which it employed were no longer acceptable to the mass of the people. To say this is not, of course, to say that it has been abolished. It can assume another form; acquire another name; reappear in a new dress. As a way of regarding people, the philosophy of the poor law is deeply embedded in the structure of English society* (Titmuss 1954).

The motivation to develop and retain segregated forms of care arose from parsimonious considerations in relation to welfare expenditure. It also reflected the prevailing attitude of the day that disabled people should be the deserving recipients of the benevolence. As Titmuss warned, Poor Law attitudes could be continually reconstructed. In 1948, Group Captain Leonard Cheshire formed the Cheshire Foundation with the aim of providing homes and employment for disabled ex-servicemen. Campbell and Oliver (1996) describe the ensuing debate over whether their efforts should be targeted at building accessible homes or the provision of nursing homes. They settled on the latter with the availability of government funding for that purpose and because they felt that the provision of a total environment in which the *men* could both live and work would be of more help to them. However, within 20 years, any gratitude which may have been present turned to resentment, particularly amongst the newer and younger residents of these institutions. Paul Hunt, who lived in one of the Cheshire Homes and felt his life devalued by his segregation, wrote to *The Guardian* in 1968 trying to make contact with other disabled people who might have similar feelings. The disabled people's movement thus became an organised activity and along with it came an analysis of disability that was to challenge the nature of the Welfare State.

Professionals and dependency
Within the individual model of disability, it is assumed that not only is disability a personal tragedy (Oliver, 1983) but also that there is a clear role for professionals in amelioration of societal disadvantagement caused by impairment. Under the social model, however (*ibid.*), the role of professionals is more part of the problem than the solution. Emphasis in the social model moves away from piecemeal strategies to ameliorate the discomforts caused by impairment (for so long a traditional central focus for professionals and one which reinforces

individualisation of the experience of disability) towards an appreciation of the adaptation required by mainstream society, its structures and institutions.

With the modern conceptualisation of disability focusing upon social, economic, and political restriction (Oliver 1990) there also developed a critical appraisal of professionalism – most specifically, the role of those professionals who work with disabled clients and the vested interests within the continuation of an unequal but State-mandated relationship. In practical terms, this is highlighted in the struggles of disabled people who, utilising the social model of disability, have pointed out that the definition of 'social need' developed by Bradshaw (1972) is merely the concern of professionals who have their own agendas within the debates around simple amelioration of the lot of disabled people (Oliver, 1990). Instead, disabled people have insisted on the right to self-definition of their needs and fought for policy changes to recognise their rights to participate as full members of society.

The types of solution to the dilemma of professional interests proposed by social model analysts place the emphasis upon social policy makers – and wider society in general – to understand the diverse social needs of *all* citizens and to take responsibility for amelioration. The appointment of 'experts' (professionals) to 'case-work' disabled people was exposed by such analysts as patriarchal and oppressive since it perpetuated dependency and simultaneously denied disabled people a 'voice'. The degree to which there has been a change can be judged by the achievement of the right of disabled people to receive direct payments to themselves to meet their own needs for assistance. In fact, the debate had centred less upon the *need* for the direct payment itself and more upon the question of why the State was refusing to recognise the *right*:

> *Under the traditional Welfare State, local authorities could only provide services or contract them to other providers; the provision of cash rather than services was illegal, even if a few imaginative authorities, in combination with disabled people and emergent user-led organisations, began to ignore the law. Moreover, the widespread dissatisfaction with provider-led professionally dominated provision within the disabled population led directly to increasingly vociferous demands from disabled people and their organisations for meaningful control of the services on which they were forced to depend* (Oliver and Barnes 1998.9).

This brief review of the historical context within which welfare provision for disabled people arose serves to highlight the paternalism and professional expert determinism so characteristic even a decade ago. It is indeed only with hindsight that we can appreciate the chicken and egg nature of the professionalisation of social need and how professionals came to be seen more as part of the problem than the solution.

Professional dependency creation

Over time, therefore, the professionals were able to develop instrumentally their notion of needs assessments for the purposes of enhancing their own professional status. As Oliver and Sapey (1999) state in relation to organisational concerns within social work practice with disabled people in 1983:

> *The organisational concerns were threefold; first that social workers act as arbiters of need between disabled people and the state; second that the responsibilities for services to disabled people were uncoordinated and distributed between a large number of organisations and rehabilitation professions; and finally the services that were available tended to reflect the professional interests and aspirations of those workers rather than being based on any analysis of disability and the needs of disabled people* (Oliver and Sapey 1999: 160).

Herein lies the paradox of a conceptualisation of social need which has a professionalised solution. The professionals, once appointed, realised that disabled people were forced to depend upon them, not least as gate-keepers to services. At the same time, both disabled people and some professionals became aware that such dependency was unhelpful and frequently unhealthy.

Professionalised service provisions within a needs-based system of welfare have added to existing forms of discrimination and have also created new forms of their own, including the provision of stigmatised segregated services such as day care and the development of professional assessments and practices based on invasions of privacy as well as creating a language of paternalism which can only enhance discriminatory practices. This situation has been exacerbated by countries like Britain exporting these professionally dominated needs-led models of welfare to parts of the developing world (Oliver and Barnes. 1998: 49).

However, to openly acknowledge that professionalised services are dependency- creating would result in the diminution of the professionals' power and status. To date, the solutions to this logical half-Nelson which have been proposed by disabled activists such as Finkelstein have not resulted in a rush of enthusiasm from professionals:

The basis of professional practice must rest on an assumption of integration and a commitment to promoting control by disabled people over their own lives. Since the lives of disabled people also depend on the actions of helpers, control over education, training and role of such helpers needs to be vested in disabled people (quite aside from the need for more disabled people to enter the profession). What this means in practice is that the role of the professional worker in rehabilitation, for example, needs to change from management of the patient to that of being a resource for the patient to use in reaching his or her own goals. The suggestions that professional workers in rehabilitation should become a resource to be utilised by disabled people is not a suggestion that professionals should become passive and all the onus for innovation, assessment, decision making etc. should fall on the shoulders of disabled people. Professionals acting as a resource to be used by others need special education and training so that they are able to promote control by disabled people (Finkelstein, 1981: 26).

Indeed it is the last issue referred to by Finkelstein here that constitutes the nub of the problem. Finkelstein, in a very telling fashion, is calling for 'special education and training' for professionals in order to orient them to the fact that disabled people should in fact be 'in control'. This call in itself exposes the fact that *traditional* service provision models serve to educate professionals to take and exercise control. However, 'control' raises the issue of professional status which has traditionally been founded on the ability and mandate to exercise power over others. Finkelstein's proposal, therefore, threatens the status and power of professionals and although it is most certainly what is required, it is unlikely to form the basis for the services of the future. However, it is also unlikely that the hegemony of the professionals and consequent dependency-creation will remain intact and the experiences gained in the struggle for direct payments will serve to justify the position of the disability movement in constantly exposing insidious practices. Instead of a complete reappraisal and reorientation, following Finkelstein (1981), or a retrenchment into professional hegemony, we are likely to see a 'mixed economy' emerging within which all solutions are *possible*, but none totally dominate provision. Social rented housing is a microcosm of these debates and changes and will be developed here to illustrate those points. Gaining access to social rented housing involves an assessment of housing need by all sorts of 'experts': allocation and tenancy officers and corroboration of needs identified by other experts, typically health and social work professionals, clearly operating on non-social model criteria. Also, and of increasing importance, it will involve determination of eligibility and entitlement to social security in order to pay the rent. Hence professional experts 'control' disabled people and create a dependency relationship in two areas of basic human needs: somewhere to live and means of subsistence.

Housing: satisfying need without rights

Social rented housing is of significance to disabled people. It is the only sector which provides dwellings which are meant for, or 'specially provided for', or adapted to the needs of - disabled people. That is a matter of policy. There may not be enough 'mobility homes' or 'wheelchair' housing. It may not be where it is needed, but it is a matter of housing policy that there should be some. Disabled people have access to it on grounds of their housing needs, rather than income. Most disabled people would not be able to afford owner-occupied property adapted to those standards.

The 'special needs' housing which we now have derives mainly from the interpretation of the Chronically Sick and Disabled Persons Act 1970 to be found in DoE Circular 74/74. It favoured an individualised dependency model, providing either customised wheelchair dwellings or 'mobility housing'. The needs of disabled people were viewed as special – and hence separate. The dwellings for them were to be of a different standard from dwellings for non-disabled people. The alternative approach would have been to build all homes to an accessible standard: 25 years later we have at last embarked on that more fruitful line of provision, underpinned if not actually inspired by the social model of disability; we are going to build Lifetime homes.

It is encouraging that the Government now support the provision of Lifetime homes, but it should be borne in mind that we are starting from almost a nil base. It will take a generation or more before there are appreciable numbers of such residential properties available. Although in the future finding housing which was built to accessible standards should be easier, in the meantime we have to rely on the mobility standard homes and wheelchair standard dwellings which have already been built. Using the Housing Investment Programme returns it can be shown that 29,932 wheelchair homes had been built and adapted by 1995, whilst in addition there are 57,268 'other dwellings for disabled people' which were not wheelchair housing. Whether that figure is sufficient depends on normative notions of need, over which there is considerable disagreement (Stewart, Harris and Sapey, 1999). We have 'estimated' the need for wheelchair dwellings to be of the order of 40,600, whilst that for mobility housing is about 69,000 (the basis of such estimates is highly problematic as is discussed in Harris, Sapey and Stewart, 1997).

91

As there are only about 30,000 wheelchair dwellings to absorb the pressure of demand from all wheelchair users in the country, it would seem reasonable to expect that they are all occupied by wheelchair users. However, a large proportion of wheelchair dwellings are occupied by households with no wheelchair users. Even when wheelchair dwellings were being introduced housing managers predicted that the provision of such specialist dwellings would lead to under-occupation by the very people for whom it was intended (MHLG, 1969: para. 114).

We have analysed the detailed allocation records of housing associations (CORE data). It can be shown that in new allocations of tenancies for 1997-8 only 23% of wheelchair-user households who became tenants were in fact allocated wheelchair properties: 6,405 tenancies of wheelchair dwellings were allocated in 1997-8 in total; of these 4,750, or 74.2%, did not have a wheelchair user in the household. The gross disparity between the intended and actual use of these newly available dwellings demands some explanation. On the face of it there appears to be a mismatch, but whether this is because of management issues or the applicants' preferences in conjunction with location, size, type, or cost of the wheelchair dwellings we do not yet know.

Commentators have suggested a number of explanations. One suggestion has been the preponderance of one-bedroomed dwellings as wheelchair homes (60% of newly allocated tenancies to wheelchair dwellings are one bedroomed); another has been that the concentration of specialist facilities on one site is rejected by many disabled people. Curiously one-bedroomed wheelchair dwellings are less likely to be allocated to a household with a wheelchair user than are three-bedroomed ones. A third explanation could be connected with the painfully slow development of co-operation between housing and social services. RADAR has noted that housing tend to rely on social services to identify the housing needs of disabled people, whilst for their part, social services do not do housing assessments.

We all know that during the period of Thatcherism public sector house-building declined; however 'special needs' housing increased during the 1980s from a fifth to a third of that declining number of completed public sector dwellings. Dwellings for disabled people were an ever larger proportion of the public sector homes actually built. Concurrently housing associations grew in importance as social landlords, by new building (20,000 p.a.), adaptations, and the transfer to them of some 277,000 local authority dwellings by the end of 1997. Hence housing associations now take the lead in the provision of wheelchair dwellings and other housing for disabled people.

The proportion of social rented sector tenants who identify themselves as 'permanently sick or disabled' has been increasing steadily until it is now about 9% of all tenants, whilst the other sectors have stayed the same. If social rented housing offers the only real opportunity for disabled people to live in appropriately adapted housing, and if supply met demand, what is the problem? Financing is the problem. Housing association grant has been lowered (as part of the move away from 'bricks and mortar' subsidies to individualised means tests). Housing associations are faced with either using reserves or borrowing more heavily.

In order to meet their costs housing associations can increase rents. As the vast majority of social rented tenants were already on Housing Benefit, the burden of increased rents falls on that part of the social security budget. Housing association rents were on average £52 per week, that is £11 a week higher than local authority rents in 1997. These higher rent levels led to a greater concentration of economically inactive and benefit-dependent households in the housing association sector – amongst whom are many disabled people. To improve their housing position disabled people must seek social rented housing and, it might be argued, in order to pay for it, have to be on Housing Benefit.

We are constantly informed by the current government that work is the answer to the iniquities of dependency, and by this they mean regular paid work (standard formulation in Secretary of State for Social Security, 1998, chap. 3). About 46% of the disabled people (within the economically active age bands) in the most recent DfEE survey were in work (1998). Their average take-home pay was £196 per week. That is slightly lower than the non-disabled average take-home pay of £212, but 45% of these disabled workers were also receiving a state benefit. What we lack is survey evidence on disabled people with which we can establish links between earnings – benefit income – housing costs and tenure. What we may be allowed to tentatively infer from the available data is that disabled people are more likely to live in social rented housing – though not necessarily appropriately allocated adapted property – and that they are likely to be on Housing Benefit, as well as receiving the range of disability benefits.

Dwellings suitable for disabled people are more expensive than 'ordinary' housing: that was the orthodoxy. Indeed housing associations had a 'multiplier' applied to their total building cost indicator for the area when providing dwellings for the disabled. The subsidy has been reduced. To stay solvent what housing associations are not supposed to do is charge tenants in costly wheelchair housing higher rents than other tenants. It is not possible to quantify the level to which this is going on. At the moment, disabled tenants claiming Housing Benefits are protected from regulations about maximum rent levels, entitlement, and pressure to move and share accommodation if single. Disabled people should not be both forced into this benefit dependency and then pilloried for being there.

The housing need of disabled people now seems more likely to be expressed in what rent level they can afford or their eligibility for maximum Housing Benefit. This question of housing need as expressed by the 'experts' versus demand from the users, and the problems of either higher bricks-and-mortar subsidies or higher rents (with ever higher HB entitlement) is most elegantly solved by Lifetime homes. The costings are comparable with general needs housing. The point is new building is going to have to conform to basic accessibility standards, but it is also carried out with the possibility of being easy to adapt to a much higher level of mobility should the need arise at a later date. Lifetime homes can be thought of as universalist – anyone can occupy them. They neither stigmatise nor create dependency. The decision to adapt fully can still be related to individual needs.

Obviously it will take generations for there to be a significant stock of Lifetime homes, but something else is looming far sooner – indeed by 2003. The Government propose that by that date Housing Benefit will exclude all aspects of housing support costs (DETR, 1998). At the moment all kinds of support may be charged against Housing Benefit and the Housing Revenue Account including 'assistance' of various kinds (from arranging plumbers to budgeting advice); settling disputes, resettlement, lifeskills training; negotiating access to professionals; shopping; counselling; monitoring alarms; cleaning tenant's rooms; providing and running restaurants, and so on.

In future central government will allocate money to local authorities who will corporately decide how it should be spent locally on support services for the vulnerable, identified as: older people; people with learning disabilities, mental health problems; victims of domestic violence; vulnerable young people; people with an alcohol or drug addiction, and ex-offenders. Disabled people are not specifically identified. In reality it seems likely that by 2003 support costs will be the responsibility of social services departments, presumably operationalised by their purchasing officers on an individual needs basis.

On the face of it this should not significantly affect disabled people in terms of their *housing* needs because those costs ought to be wholly covered by Housing Benefit. The contested area will be on-site provisions such as most of those listed above and here disabled people will have to compete with those other service-user groups. Our point here could well be: why should disabled people pursuing the social model bother to engage with this further extension of professionalised need-determination, and do so in competition with other vulnerable groups? The answer will turn on how far the administration of this measure erodes the cover which Housing Benefit affords the total rent.

In terms of new build or adaptation schemes in line with the Lifetime homes principle, there should be no disincentive to new initiatives as the whole idea rests on physical, built features, not services. The difficult issues reside in the purchase and provision of supportive services are established. It could be argued that the uncertainty is a disincentive to *schemes* of housing for disabled people as the costings for services of support would in future have a less certain funding. Disability rights activists should not on the face of it be too concerned, as they tend to reject such specialist provision. However, the list of 'experts' who know what disabled people should have lengthens and widens from the individualised needs assessment by housing professionals, social security adjudication officers, to social services purchasing managers – over the one issue, living independently in one's own (socially rented) home.

New Labour, new dependency
As we pointed out in the introduction, the pursuit of rights and entitlements is but one tactic in the general strategy to emancipate disabled people from the medical model. We have noted how 'special needs' housing delivered disabled people into the hands of professionalised needs assessors. The solution of Lifetime homes will be slow, but is now also tinged with concern around Housing Benefit and support costs. The concept of Lifetime homes suggests a *reduction* in dependency and individualised 'expert' need assessment, the *Supporting People* Housing Benefit initiative an *increase*. But there is another far more generalised area of dependency construction to be analysed: social security. The New Deal for disabled people announced by the Government in July 1998 is intended to 'boost the job chances' of disabled people. It is envisaged that this will be done by:

- providing active tailored help and encouragement to move into work
- sweeping away obstacles to work in the benefits and rules system
- ensuring work pays via introduction of minimum wage
- tackling discrimination in work place.

(Social Security Press Release 9.8.98)

These tactics are intended to provide 'a hand up not a hand out' as part of the 'Welfare to Work' programme. It is too early to assess whether or not the Government will be successful in this strategy. However, it is noticeable that the underlying message of the strategy can be seen as part of a moral crusade by government ministers to disparage those who take such 'hand outs', for behind the measured tones of principle number one of the government's reform programme– 'The new Welfare State should help and encourage people of working age to work where they are capable of doing so' (Secretary of State for Social Security, 1998: 2) – it is clear that this means everybody (single parents having been singled out as a notable case for treatment). It is curious and ironic that it should be a Labour government which is doing this, when its predecessors actually created the rights and entitlements to benefit now under attack. As we have noted, (Stewart *et al.*, 1999) the disparagement of disabled people constitutes a removal of their previous 'deserving' status. This status, although challenged in minor ways by previous administrations, has never before been subjected to full-scale attack. It would appear that the motive is part of an effort by New Labour to be 'even-handed' with all welfare recipients. We should also note at this juncture that the tenets of the social model of disability support the idea of removal of 'deserving' status, arguing instead for a rights base for welfare provision, thereby dispensing with any judgements which might be made on a basis of favouritism. The long history of disabled people as 'objects of charity' (and their utter rejection of the same) forms a crucial part of this debate. So, in many crucial respects the disability rights movement may support the spirit of the changes heralded by the New Deal and we may be tempted to ask whether justice has been done at last.

As social policy analysts, our endorsement of the general trends would depend upon the extent to which the Government can achieve serious recognition of disabled people's particular aspirations in regard to employment and, most importantly, the political will to support challenges that will arise within the workplace should the anticipated rise in disabled people's employment take place. This would require a wholesale assault on structural discrimination on a national scale: tackling disincentives to work and removing the real barriers to employment. These are complicated issues which will require careful monitoring if they are to achieve the desired outcomes.

Leaving on one side for a moment this monumental task, if we look broadly at the strategy as a whole it is apparent that the New Deal gives disabled people equal status with many other groups currently challenging inequalities and social exclusion: black and minority ethnic groups; single parents. However, it is not a level playing field out there and in many respects the old 'deserving' status recognised this. Put differently, although all of these groups share oppression by the majority, some have more resources than others to fight back. Historically, the 'deserving' status accorded to disabled people formed part of societal recognition of this lack of equity between the minorities (albeit delivered within a patronising format). However, by 'eschewing charitable and discretionary welfare for rights entitlements, disabled people have placed themselves in the rough-house of party politics' (Stewart *et al.*, 1999). This 'rough-house' is likely to prove to be exactly as it sounds in the coming months and years.

Conclusion
We have argued that dependency is perceived and experienced as a negative state and that welfare responses have often been to reinforce that dependency. We have seen how professionals carved for themselves a role in both defining and ameliorating social need. For a considerable period of our history, disabled people have been subjected to their solutions, until the innovation of the social model of disability exposed their vested interests. In fact it took the radical focus of the social model of disability to expose the role of the professional in the *creation* of social need, which before this date had appeared wholly unremarkable and indeed necessary to all concerned parties.

In the area of housing, the agendas of successive Conservative administrations have been to reduce government subsidies on building homes. This has been done without regard for the impact it may have on various groups of people, including the disabled. The past 20 years have seen an increase in dependency due to housing policy despite the increase in the numbers of disabled people leaving institutions. The New Deal from the current Labour administration is yet to do more than reopen the 'sheltered workshop' approach to employment for disabled people which will further reinforce this level of dependency.

Radical solutions to the dilemma of professional control and dependency-creation have been proposed by disabled activists (Finkelstein 1981). However, as we have shown, these are unlikely to appeal to the professionals. It is clear that there can be no return to the past professional hegemony either and a 'mixed economy' in which power and decision-making is a shared endeavour is more likely to form the basis of future service provision.

References

Bradshaw, J (1972) 'The concept of social need' *New Society* 30 March pp 640 –43

Campbell, J and Oliver, M (1996) *Disability Politics: Understanding Our Past, Changing Our Future* Routledge, London

Department of the Environment, Transport and the Regions (1998) *Supporting People: a new policy and funding framework for support services* The Stationery Office, London

Finkelstein, V (1981) *Disability & Professional Attitudes* NAIDEX Convention, Sevenoaks

Harris, J, Sapey, B and Stewart, J (1997) *Wheelchair Housing and the Estimation of Need* UCLAN/NATWHAG, Preston

Labour Party 1998 *The Views of the Labour Party* www/labour.org.uk/views/index.html

Ministry of Housing and Local Government (1969) *Council Housing, Purposes, Procedures and Priorities* (Cullingworth chair) London, HMSO

Oliver, M (1983) *Social Work with Disabled People* Macmillan, Basingstoke

Oliver, M (1990) *The Politics of Disablement* Macmillan, Basingstoke

Oliver, M (1996) *Understanding disability: from theory to practice* Macmillan, Basingstoke

Oliver M and Barnes C (1998) *Disabled People and Social Policy: From Exclusion to Inclusion* Longman, London

Oliver M and Sapey B (1999) *Social Work with Disabled People* (2nd edition) Macmillan, Basingstoke

Secretary of State for Social Security and the Minister for Welfare Reform (1998) *New Ambitions for Our Country: a new contract for welfare* Cm. 3805, The Stationery Office, London

Stewart, J, Harris, J and Sapey, B (1999) 'Disability and Dependency: origins and futures of "special needs" housing for disabled people' *Disability and Society* vol. 14, no. 1, pp 5–20

Titmuss R M (1954) 'The administrative setting of social service: some historical reflections' *Case Conference* vol., no. 1, pp 15-11

Chapter 9
Community Care, Community Work and Social Exclusion
Peter Sharkey

This chapter takes three topics – social exclusion, community care, and community work – and explores some of the links and connections between them. It argues for a community care practice which is reinvigorated through the application of community work principles and which can make connections to the issues of social exclusion which are now on the political agenda.

It was the National Health Service and Community Care Act 1990 which set the direction of community care developments in the 1990s. With origins in the Griffiths Report (1988) and the White Paper, Caring For People (DoH, 1989), the Act laid the platform for current community care practice. Particular emphasis within the changes has been on the purchaser/provider split, care management, and the development and operation of 'eligibility criteria' for services. Considerable variation in charges and services between local authorities has developed (DoH, 1998). Community care policies and finance developed under a New Right framework have targeted those individuals 'with greatest needs' (DoH, 1989, 1.10) and this shift to targeting has been effective (DoH, 1997).

Throughout these developments, few connections were made between community care practice and community work. Historically, community work has at times had a close relationship with social work. However, community work skills and practice have not been perceived as relevant to the increasingly individualistic community care philosophy and practice of the 1990s. This chapter argues for a closer relationship between community work approaches and community care.

The concept of social exclusion, originating in France during the 1970s, has been used within the European Union during the 1980s and 1990s and was adopted by New Labour politicians in the late-1990s. Poverty was effectively off the agenda of politics for the whole of the 18 years of Conservative government, even though poverty and inequality increased (Hills, 1995). The change to a Labour government in 1997 resulted in the language of social exclusion and poverty becoming a central part of political discourses. Social exclusion has become a concept which has broad acceptance both within the UK and continental Europe (Madanipour *et al.*, 1998) probably because it means different things to different people.

The links between community care users and those socially excluded are manifest. Few sectors of society can be more excluded than homeless people and drug abusers. Anyone studying the experiences of people with learning difficulties or mental health problems during this century and last would be struck by the 'exclusion' they had suffered in different ways. There were no greater symbols of exclusion than the large hospitals on the outskirts of towns built to separate those who were different.

Social exclusion

There are differing interpretations of what social exclusion is and Levitas (1998) distinguishes between three competing discourses which she labels as RED, MUD, and SID. RED is a redistributionist discourse in which social exclusion is concerned with poverty and structural inequality. MUD (the moral underclass discourse) uses cultural explanations of poverty and tends to blame the poor for their poverty. SID (social integrationist discourse) emphasises paid work and integration within the labour market. Levitas comments, 'To oversimplify, in RED they have no money, in SID they have no work, in MUD they have no morals (1998, p. 27)'. Levitas argues that Labour had largely operated an inconsistent combination of SID and MUD. In its first annual report on 'Tackling Poverty and Social Exclusion' (DSS, 1999) the Government seems to slide between all three models. In considering their own role and position in relation to social exclusion it is important for community care workers to keep in mind the three models or discourses. MUD takes us back to blaming the poor whilst RED and SID focus on poverty and the structural and labour market inequalities.

Tackling social exclusion has been a central element of the Labour Government's policies. In each part of the UK strategies have been set in place. In England the Social Exclusion Unit (SEU) was set up in December 1997, based in the Cabinet Office and reporting directly to the Prime Minister. It was a modest initiative. The unit consisted of only 12 people, with no budget of its own, and with an initial life span of only two years (Halpern, 1998). In its early months it was given the brief to focus on three areas – truancy, homelessness, and neighbourhood renewal (the fourth New Deal). The latter two had direct relevance to community care: £800 million was set aside for deprived communities and £145 million for rough sleeping in London, £34 million for homelessness elsewhere. There was an ambitious target of cutting homelessness by two-thirds by the year 2002.

The fourth New Deal was launched in September 1998. This was the 'New Deal For Communities', backed by £800 million to tackle problems on England's worst estates. The background and proposals were published in a report from the Social Exclusion Unit (1998). Initially money was to be spent on 17 local authority 'pathway' pilot areas. This number was to be expanded later but the plan set out was that by the end of 1999 the Government would have produced a 10- to 20-year plan to turn round deprived neighbourhoods, to reduce dependency, and empower local communities to shape a better future for themselves (SEU, 1998).

A problem which many regeneration projects have stressed is that the mainstream public services in poor neighbourhoods are frequently ineffective (SEU, 1998, p 10). In spite of many demands for mainstream programmes to be 'bent' towards the needs of poor areas, there is little evidence that this happens (SEU, 1998, p 38). The issue here is for social services departments to bend their provision towards poor areas and to use their resources in an imaginative way. There is a need to analyse the problems, understand what the Government is trying to do with area-based projects, and work with the policies rather than against them. A key point is that the mainstream welfare services can encourage and create exclusion or inclusion. As Parkinson has written, 'Explicit urban strategies can make a difference, but mainstream programmes make a greater one' (Parkinson, 1998, p 34). Thus mainstream policies and practices within social work and community care need to change.

The SEU report noted the need for the involvement of local people and the need for community development to be a central part of the regeneration strategy, saying that 'it has become conventional wisdom that communities need to be involved both in designing what is to be done and in implementing it, and that the best policies work through genuine partnerships' (SEU, 1998, p 34). This has repeatedly been said by government and the report on 'Tackling Poverty and Social Exclusion' emphasised that one of the three key themes central to the whole approach was 'the involvement of local people and community organisations' (DSS, 1999, p 145).

For workers in mainstream programmes such as community care it is important that they are aware of and involved in the local regeneration strategy. Given that it is acknowledged that, to be successful, regeneration requires local participation then it follows that community care activities in an area should be participative and collective. In reality they are often the very opposite to this. 'Tackling Poverty and Social Exclusion' (DSS, 1999) has a focus on many of the excluded groups which are often central to social work practice – with coverage of disabled people, people with mental health problems, carers, rough sleepers, drug misusers, older people, and people in the very poorest communities – and yet social work has limited mention as having any response in terms of tackling exclusion.

Mutual aid and self-help are seen as crucial to addressing the issues of poverty, exclusion, and regeneration (Burns and Taylor, 1998). New Labour has had some emphasis on both communitarian ideas and mutual aid. Thus community work strategies and skills have much to offer in relation to tackling social exclusion. If community care work is to make a contribution in this area then it needs to break free from the 'individualistic' philosophy of the Thatcher years and to draw from the community work traditions within social work. Community work has a history of both tackling social divisions and working to empower people (Mayo, 1998). There is much to be said for community care work to draw on community work skills and approaches and we shall explore next the ways in which this might be done.

The contribution of community work

Central to community work has always been an emphasis on the importance of the values of collective organisation and participation. Tracing back the history of both community and social work, there have been periods when both traditions have come close together and periods when they have been more separated. Views vary on the origins of community work but one writer describes the Church of England parish priest Samuel Barnett as 'the man who has the best claim to be considered the first British community worker' (Baldock, 1980, p. 30). Barnett was very active within the Charity Organisation Society (COS) but found it increasingly difficult to justify the division of people into the deserving and undeserving poor. The roots of social work are often described as being in the nineteenth-century COS. Barnett and others argued that many problems had wider environmental causes and that there was a need for collective action. Barnett became instrumental in the setting up of Toynbee Hall as the first settlement in 1884. Other settlements followed and a key element of the settlement movement was living and working in the same area. Settlements have played and continue to play an important role in the development and practice of community work. During this period of history aspects of social work and community held together under COS and then split apart into the separate strands of COS and the settlements.

Thus going back into the nineteenth-century, practitioners (using different language) were grappling with differing perceptions of the causes of poverty (individual or structural), issues of empowerment, and issues of anti-oppressive practice (at least in terms of practice which tackled environmental and structural poverty).

With the development of community care practice during the 1990s, one can see similarities with the differing perceptions of the causes of poverty which were involved in the split in the 1880s. Influenced by New Right ideas there has been an intense individualising process in the way community care has been implemented. A decision has to be made as to whether someone receives a comprehensive assessment. If they do then their needs have to be set against 'eligibility criteria'. This 'targeting those in greatest need' can operate in ways which are not dissimilar to the processes of dividing people into the deserving and undeserving poor operated by the Charity Organisation Society. The move towards individualising need feeds into a process of 'pathologising' – the person is a problem and by and large it is their own fault that they are a problem. There are strong echoes here of the Moral Underclass Discourse (MUD) and from here it is a small step back to the notion of deserving and undeserving poor so prevalent in the nineteenth century. We have lost some of the sense of structural (or society based) causes of problems which people like Samuel Barnett pointed to (with echoes of SID and RED in that perspective).

The potential links between social work and community work have been revisited at different times. Social work was reorganised as a result of the Seebohm Report of 1968 which stressed the need for the new departments to link into their local communities. Community work was seen to have a role within departments during the 1970s. Many departments responded to Seebohm by having one community worker attached to each area team. Following on from the Barclay Report (1982) there was a brief flourishing of 'community social work' initiatives. There were some imaginative and exciting attempts to merge social work and community work (Darvil and Smale, 1990). However, these innovations were marginalised by child care scandals, two major pieces of legislation (the Children Act 1989 and the National Health Service and Community Care Act 1990), the subsequent division within most departments (usually into Children/Families and Adults), and the purchaser:provider split. All of these developments resulted in the development of structures which made it harder to operate community social work, which seemed to thrive best in devolved structures where generic workers could be clearly identified with a particular area.

The individualistic approach continued apace. In the Department of Health's guidance for practitioners on the community care changes (DoH, 1991) there is no mention of a community approach. The emphasis was on setting up individual care management, individual assessment, individual care plans, and individual packages of care.

Yet there are powerful arguments for questioning this development and for developing a much closer relationship between community work and community care (Sharkey, 2000, Barr *et al.*, 1997). In particular within the changes there has been a considerable emphasis on user-empowerment. In order to translate this rhetoric of empowerment into practice and link it to the ideas of anti-oppressive practice (CCETSW, 1995), community care practice needs to look to community work for ideas.

Firstly, the vast proportion of community care is done by informal carers. These are people in the community who are the natural constituency of community workers. Community workers are experts at the work of crossing boundaries between sectors and making links between different groups and different people. The 1985 General Household Survey was the first large-scale study to include detailed information on Britain's carers. The study showed that there are six million carers in the United Kingdom: one adult in seven is a carer; 15% of all adult women are carers; 12% of all adult men are carers; and 3% of adults in the UK (about 1.4 million people) devote at least 20 hours per week to caring (Green, 1988). With such numbers, it is the community work skills of facilitation, empowerment, networking, and working with groups and collectivities which are centrally relevant to community care work.

Secondly, community work techniques can contribute to difficult local situations. Some of the dilemmas of community care provision are familiar and have not been dealt with well. What do you do, for example, if a local community group vociferously objects to the setting up of a small home for say three people with learning difficulties in the neighbourhood? There are no easy answers but community work has often grappled with situations like this where there is a conflict between the demands of a group and personal/professional values. Community work has a real contribution in helping to develop anti-oppressive practice in such situations.

Thirdly, there is the role for community work skills in helping to make community care schemes work. The movement from institution to the community for many has been a movement to increased isolation, loneliness, and despair. This need not be so and indeed there have been good schemes where this has not been the case. Any successful scheme which achieves some social inclusion has to involve the local community in some way. People discharged from hospital after many years frequently have their social networks fractured. Careful work has to be done to build new ones (and keep some links to old ones) and this involves links to the informal networks in the new area – these are often simply the links of friendship and recognition (rather than antagonism and hostility) which are crucial to a new way of life.

Fourthly, there are the contributions of community work to self-help and political change. Consider, for example, this often-quoted extract from the White Paper, Growing Older:

Whatever level of public expenditure proves practicable and however it is distributed, the primary sources of support and care for elderly people are informal and voluntary. These spring from personal ties of kinship, friendship and neighbourhood. They are irreplaceable. It is the role of public authorities to sustain and where necessary develop – but never to displace – such support and care. Care in the community must increasingly mean care by the community (DHSS, 1981.)

Most community care will always be 'by' the community and community work skills have a role in maximising the effectiveness of this. However, the above quotation (with the stress on 'by' the community) presents the potential problem for both community care workers and community workers of being part of the process of letting public authorities ease out of their responsibilities. Here again the organising and lobbying skills associated with community work skills can help to ensure that the public authorities meet their own responsibilities.

Some service users have shown their own dislike for the community care changes and shown the way themselves with or without community work help. In parts of Cheshire, for example, the community care changes led to increases in charges on a number of services. Carers' groups in the county lobbied hard and took effective 'action' to modify these charges. There has been a growth of disabled people's groups which have campaigned and taken 'action' on different aspects of policy and provision. Many of their concerns have been about community care issues – appropriate transport, access to buildings, freedom from discrimination in housing and employment, the right to employ your own carer rather than have one imposed upon you. It has become clear that community care is a fertile ground for people coming together, recognising their common problems, and working out a strategy to improve the situation (Shaw, 1996).

Groups have often taken their own action and shown what can be done. Look for example at the history of the self-advocacy movement amongst people with learning disabilities as outlined in 'We Can Speak For Ourselves' (Williams and Shoultz, 1982). Groups involved with community care provision have fought in different ways against stigma, oppression, and poor services. Some of the most memorable 'direct action' during the early 1990s involved disabled people campaigning for civil rights legislation. As Petrie suggests, community workers have much to learn from disability politics and disabled people's organisations (Petrie, 1996). The same can be said in relation to community care workers.

Breaking free from the individualistic approach in community care
Social workers (or care managers) in community care talk of a low morale, a loss of the social work role because they are concerned with assessment, and an excess of paperwork (Hadley and Clough, 1996). Community care workers have found it difficult to do other than accept the system of operation which has been given to them. There are some positives. The community care changes have given attention to some neglected and socially excluded groups of people. As the 1990s progressed the weaknesses of the 1990 community care legislation became clearer. Some of the faults had to be addressed by piecemeal legislation concerning carers, independent living, and discrimination against disabled people. The Labour Government has introduced a White Paper which is about modernising social care (DoH, 1998). However, more needs to be done to break free from the strait-jacket of the individualistic approach with its links to individualising explanations of poverty and, with tight resources, its perceived and felt divisions into those who are deserving of help and those who are not. Whilst it is true that the Government has not stressed the role of social work in relation to tackling exclusion, the White Paper does give a clear invitation to be involve: 'More widely, social services can make an important contribution to wider local authority-led programmes to tackle the problems of homelessness, poor housing conditions, and social exclusion in deprived neighbourhoods. These issues, and the need for coordinated local approaches to tackle them, have been covered in the Social Exclusion Unit's reports on rough sleepers and on Neighbourhood renewal' (DoH. 1998, 6.23).

Barr *et al.*, have developed a training pack which identifies the contribution that active engagement with communities can make to the development of effective community care. They write: 'Following the National Health Service and Community Care Act 1990, community care policy has done little to explore the potential and limitations of neighbourhoods as the context for the provision of care. Equally, the potential for treating care user groups as communities of common interest, who can be supported to take action on their own needs, has scarcely been addressed. Yet these are key issues' (1997, p. vii).

They argue that the values of community care and community development are very similar. These similar values are identified as participation, needs-led partnership, social inclusion, and empowerment. The training pack has some case studies which show how community development can take forward user involvement and participation and make clear links between user groups and the wider society. They write, 'Social work, health and other professionals have embraced the concepts of empowerment, participation, partnership, social inclusion and anti-discriminatory practice. Yet much of their practice is located in a paradigm which cannot see beyond individual assessment and care planning. This myopia constrains the application of these concepts which find their real potential in collective action by and with communities to meet their own needs and pursue more relevant and effective services' (Barr *et al.*, 1997, p 150).

There is a long tradition of radical social work which always needs interpreting again in terms of current circumstances. Crucial to the enterprise though is avoiding pathologising, having structural rather than individual explanations, and seeking out collective responses wherever possible. In terms of Levitas's models of social exclusion, this means an emphasis on RED and a rejection of MUD.

Social exclusion and community care
Social work has traditionally been associated with the poor, the marginalised and excluded so should have some contribution in the task of tackling social exclusion. In the 1990s the individualising of community care work became the dominant organisational principle but it has been argued that by this individualising and pathologising, there has been and remains a danger of making the situation worse. Social services departments rarely have a particular response to area regeneration policies. The same policies of tight eligibility criteria still apply. 'Targeting those in greatest need' hardly contributes to a collective community endeavour.

In areas particularly identified as needing regeneration, there are often a high proportion of community care concerns. These might include, for example, high concentrations of people with mental health or drug/alcohol problems. Problems which afflict whole communities are not best responded to by individualistic responses from reactive services. Whilst there has been a history of regeneration policies going back 30 years, during the 1980s and early 1990s the emphasis of regeneration was on economic objectives and on the role of the private sector – with the aim of increasing inward investment into certain areas which were in need of regeneration. More-recent policies and approaches (SEU, 1998) have clearly included a social dimension in them. Thus recent government policies looking for community regeneration and capacity building are to be welcomed and have an important role in developing a sensible way forward in relation to community care. Community care workers can help with a shift from 'picking up the pieces' within poor areas to helping people within such areas to move forward, improve the quality of their lives, and have some say over the future of their neighbourhood.

Hoggett *et al.*, argue that most urban regeneration initiatives in London have given little attention to mental health or social issues. They note 'the marginal position of health in general and mental health in particular in urban regeneration policy' (Hoggett *et al.*, 1999, p 11). They indicate the demonstrated links that are there between mental health and poverty, unemployment, and stressful living situations.

Regeneration strategies for an area are frequently concerned with issues of direct concern to community care service users. A housing strategy needs to have supported housing central within its consideration. An employment strategy needs to have policies to assist disabled people enter the job market. Hence the importance of community care users and workers being involved directly and closely in the local development of policy. Barry and Hallett argue that social work and community care work have an important role to play in fostering social inclusion and in tackling regeneration (1998).

There is a rhetoric concerned with empowerment within the community care changes. This is frequently interpreted as individual empowerment through, for example, more information or the ability to make some limited choice. However, this rhetoric can be linked to another way of working which really tries to engage with the community and is part of a wider community empowerment. In a book on social work and exclusion all contributors argue for greater user involvement in relation to their needs and care (Barry and Hallett, 1998). It is in this area of collective user-involvement that there are particularly clear links to be made between community work, community care, and exclusion.

Conclusion

This chapter has argued that:

- ✦ Community care needs to be concerned with poverty and exclusion as a high percentage of the problems dealt with by community care workers are substantially caused by and linked to poverty and exclusion.

- Community care practice can learn much from the practice and skills of community work.

- Community work (with its traditional emphasis on participation and addressing structural inequality) is an important aspect of strategies to combat exclusion.

Poverty, deprivation, and exclusion are often used interchangeably. Increasingly exclusion is most commonly used. The Social Exclusion Unit, with very limited resources, has enabled a debate to be started about poverty and exclusion across the whole range of social policy and government departments. There is a danger of this debate missing social work and community care and it has been argued that community care workers have a role to play in relation to the discourses about social exclusion.

Social services departments hardly seem to figure in government initiatives on Sure Start (for disadvantaged children), education and health action zones, employment zones, the continuing single regeneration budget, and the national strategy for neighbourhood renewal. Many of these initiatives are attempts to prevent the sort of problems which social services departments have to deal with and yet the activity seems to be largely by-passing them.

It has also been argued that some aspects of this debate may find echoes from the beginnings of social work in the cultural explanations of poverty found within the Charity Organisation Society whilst other aspects may find echoes in the more environmental explanations of poverty espoused by Samuel Barnett and the settlement movement. These current debates on the nature of poverty and exclusion need to be engaged in by practitioners through an avoidance of pathologising and a reaffirmation of the structural causes of poverty. If practitioners are to make a difference, then they need to link up these three overlapping areas of social exclusion, community work, and community care in a climate that at least is now more open to debate and presents some opportunities which may be developed.

References
Baldock, P (1980) 'The Origins Of Community Work In The United Kingdom' in Henderson,P, Jones, D and Thomas, D N (eds) *The Boundaries Of Change In Community Work* London, Allen and Unwin, pp 25-48

Barclay Report (1982) *Social Workers: Their Role And Tasks* London, Bedford Square Press

Barr, A Drysdale J and Henderson P (1997) *Towards Caring Communities* Brighton, Pavillion

Barry, M and Hallett, C (1998) *Social Exclusion And Social Work* Lyme Regis, Russell House Publishing Ltd

Burns, D and Taylor, M (1998) *Mutual Aid And Self-Help* Bristol, Policy Press

CCETSW (1995) *Dipsw – Rules and Requirements For The Diploma In Social Work* London, CCETSW

Darvil, G and Smale, G (1990) *Partners In Empowerment: Networks of Innovation in Social Work* London, National Institute of Social Work

DHSS (1981) Growing Older London, HMSO

DoH (1989) Caring For People London, HMSO

DoH (1991) *Care Management and Assessment: Practitioners' Guide* London, HMSO

DoH (1997) *Better Management, Better Care: The Sixth Annual Report Of The Chief Inspector* London, Stationery Office

DoH (1998) *Modernising Social Services* London: Stationery Office

DSS (1999) *Opportunity For All: Tackling Poverty and Social Exclusion* London, Stationery Office

Green, H (1988) *Informal Carers* London, HMSO

Griffiths, R (1988) *Community Care: Agenda For Action* London, HMSO

Hadley, R and Clough, R (1996) *Care In Chaos* London, Cassell

Halpern, D (1998) 'Poverty, Social Exclusion and The Policy-Making Process: The Road From Theory To Practice' in Oppenheim, C (ed) *An Inclusive Society* London, IPPR, pp 269-83

Hills, J (1995) *Inquiry Into Income And Wealth Vol. 1 and 2* York, Joseph Rowntree Foundation

Hoggett, P, Stewart, M, Razzaque, K and Barker, I (1999) *Urban Regeneration And Mental Health In London* London, King's Fund

Levitas, R (1998) *The Inclusive Society?* London, Macmillan

Madanipour, A, Cars, G and Allen, J (1998) *Social Exclusion In European Cities* London, Jessica Kingsley

Mayo, M (1998) 'Community Work' in Adams, R ,Dominelli, L, Payne, M (eds) *Social Work: Themes, Issues and Critical Debates* London, Macmillan, pp 160-72

Parkinson, M (1998) *Combating Social Exclusion* Bristol, Policy Press

Petrie, M (1996) 'Disabled People And Inclusion: A Discourse Of Rights, Not Charity' in Cooke, I and Shaw, M (eds) *Radical Community Work* Edinburgh, Moray House Publications pp 103-22

Sharkey, P (2000) 'Community Work and Community Care: Links In Practice And In Education' *Journal of Social Work Education* (forthcoming)

Shaw, M (1996) 'Out Of The Quagmire: Community Care – Problems and Possibilities For Radical Practice' in Cooke, I and Shaw, M (eds) *Radical Community Work* Edinburgh, Moray House Publications, pp 85-102

SEU (1998) *Bringing Britain Together: A National Strategy For Neighbourhood Renewal* London, Stationery Office

Williams, P and Shoultz, B (1982) *We Can Speak For Ourselves* London, Souvenir Press

Chapter 10
Children and Families Social Work – Visions of the Future
Annie Huntington[1]

This chapter seeks to explore a number of interrelated themes focused on the future of social work[2] with children and their families. Although many of the themes are not new, given social work has always been contentious activity as staff manage the tensions of meditating the relationship between the child, family, and state (Parton, 1995a), the context within which they are being 'played out' may be. Historically, and whether or not social workers believe their work is 'professional' activity, staff inevitably hold a role for society as 'street level bureaucrats' (Hudson, 1993). As such they must struggle with power issues embedded in their daily activities as they work with relatively powerless people (Hugman, 1991). In the process staff have to deal with moral and ethical, not just technical, dilemmas that are an integral, not peripheral, aspect of social work practice (Hugman and Smith, 1995). Within this frame of reference balancing the care-control functions that are embedded in the role – whilst at times also attempting to effect social change through broad based interventions that do not replicate the case work focus – is, was, and probably always will be central to the role (e.g. Handler, 1968; Parton, 1997). If we forget to remember this we shall probably fail to appreciate the extent to which social workers are inevitably involved in intervening in people's lives in ways that will be contested. Not least, because social work is socially constructed activity that is affected by wider political and economic forces that shape the agenda for contemporary practice (Foren and Bailey, 1968; Payne, 1991). Social work is inevitably politicised activity as staff offer services to some of the most marginalised and disadvantaged members in society. They do this against a backdrop of changing political and public concerns and this may result in social work providers being scapegoated[3], like social work clients[4]. Particularly as any narrative of social work competence may be lost in the mêlée of competing voices that negatively assess from the outside the practice inside social work agencies. As Wise (1991) states the dominance of the most powerful voices, for example NSPCC staff who posit themselves as experts, not children, parents or core state officials (usually statutory social workers), structures analysis of social work responses in particular, at times problematic ways.

Acceptance of, and work with, the core tensions generated by the competing agendas which frame social work practice has historically been an important and inescapable aspect of practice. As Satyamurti argued in 1981, the unpredictability of social work practice, and a sense of 'unlimited liability', fundamentally shapes staff responses as they struggle with a sense of meaninglessness and minimal achievement that appears to be a perennial problem in social service departments. However, the struggle to accommodate various agendas and work creatively with core tensions embedded in the role has arguably been exacerbated in the recent past as external agendas compete and collide, messages are mixed and staff within social services departments feel the ground shifting under them at an alarming rate. Any resultant destabilisation is particularly worrying in the child care arena as it has been clearly demonstrated that staff need supportive systems if they are to deliver good-quality responses to children and their families (e.g. Richards *et al.*, 1990; Cleaver *et al.*, 1998) when occupying a difficult social role. As Cleaver and Freeman (1995) state, childcare professionals need:

> ... *the skills of Machiavelli, the wisdom of Solomon, the compassion of Augustine and the hide of a tax inspector* (p.19).

A tall order indeed and one that may be impossible to meet as staff attempt to manage the demands of their respective roles even as they accommodate changing visions of their roles and responsibilities. Whether wider structures and social or political responses facilitate or inhibit social workers, as they attempt to manage the demands of their role, is an important, and inevitably contentious, question. The presentation of issues here follows from a concern to document social workers' experiences, as their working lives change around them, and rests on empirical work undertaken within one metropolitan authority, referred to as Northtown[5], between 1995 and 1998.

Some background concerns

At the widest level the Welfare State has been restructured as the transformation begun in the Thatcher years has swept away old certainties about the role of the State, the nature of welfare provision, and the function of social services departments. Although there have clearly been challenges to the operation of the pre-Thatcher Welfare State, that rest on the articulation of problems in practice for many welfare recipients (e.g. Beresford and Croft, 1986), there has been little consensus as to the way forward (James, 1994). Not least, as the agendas of the New Right and some of the new social movements[6] may collide in criticising the past but diverge when it comes to articulating visions of the future. Despite this, and although dissenting voices have been heard, there appears to have been almost unstoppable movement to a minimal market-orientated state as a model of choice – even if this is unlikely to serve the interests of the most disadvantaged (James, 1994). The post-war consensus, if this ever existed, has been undermined (Jones and Novak, 1993; Holman ,1993) as individualised accounts of contemporary social problems, that may be linked to the 'New Victorianism' (e.g. Murray, 1994), have gained prominence. Although we can view recent changes as providing a 'window of opportunity', a space for the reconstruction of service provision in socially responsive and responsible ways that do not replicate the construction of unwieldy bureaucratic institutions (James, 1994), it is hard to see how this translates in practice (Holman, 1993). Concerns with the wider organisation and management of the welfare state continue to tax commentators as the politics of the 'Third Way' have been introduced and previous political agendas lost or carried forward – albeit under the banner of a Labour rather than a Conservative administration (Jacques, 1998). Overall, and despite a change in political administration with a wide-ranging reform agenda affecting all areas of Welfare State provision, the terrain which shapes contemporary social work practice remains fraught with tensions and contradictions.

These wider agendas clearly have more local implications, in this case in terms of the organisation of the personal social services as evidenced by the publication of recent White Papers (DoH, 1997; DoH, 1998a) which articulate changing frameworks for the delivery of services. Although differences are evident there is also continuity across the political divide as emphasis is placed on corporate work, strategic planning, seamless services, measurable outcomes, central government agendas and local government responsibility, target setting and external assessments of organisational performance (e.g. DoH 1998a; 1998b; DoH 1999a; 1999b). Most recently the Quality Protects initiative for children and families services encompasses many of these strands. As Frank Dobson (DoH,1998b) highlighted this is a major policy initiative that sets new national objectives for children's services, which must be articulated in annual Quality Protects Management Action plans if authorities are to receive associated funding. In this context local councillors have an important role in ensuring the programme is delivered successfully. These changes have implications for the organisation and management of services and follow hard on the heels of prior initiatives, particularly the NHS and Community Care Act 1990, which resulted in the reconfiguration of service provision – for example, through establishment of the purchaser/provider split. Within this context there are clearly concerns regarding the extent to

115

which the Children Act 1989, a broadly based welfare-orientated piece of legislation that enshrines a focus on participation and co-operation between parents and state employees, may or may not be implemented. As Packman and Jordan (1991) argued the Act may well founder as:

Its scope, vision and promises are large, yet history tells us that the issues it addresses will not be resolved easily (p.324).

Such concerns have been given additional weight as publication of Messages from Research (DoH 1995) has highlighted the extent to which coercive child-protection-focused interventions are said to have dominated the social work agenda in the recent past. Whether social workers, employed within statutory agencies, have a future role in terms of providing supportive interventions and/or fulfilling protective functions is debatable. The face of social work is changing and it is possible to argue that initiatives that may have previously seemed unimaginable are rapidly becoming a reality – for example, the separation out of specific investigative functions that may be performed by 'specialised teams' of police officers and social workers (DoH 1998c).

Ultimately, the only certainty seems to be that there is no certainty about the future(s) of social work – particularly as old welfare structures have been destabilised before any 'clear' alternative has emerged. Within this context staff have to cope with the daily demands of practice, even as those demands change around them. More specifically they have to cope with changing roles and responsibilities within a hostile climate that reflects the widespread operation of blame cultures in contemporary society (Parton, 1997). Unsurprisingly, exhaustion and confusion are rife as people's working lives change around them – often in ways that they neither welcome nor embrace. In the process, services to children and their families may well be negatively affected – despite the rhetoric of improving provision to ensure families in need receive the help they seek as children are protected and/or provided with appropriate alternative care when necessary.

Against this backdrop, social workers, like social work clients, deserve to have their perspective(s) articulated. Not least, as both social workers and their clients are positioned at the base of socially constructed hierarchies, albeit in differing ways and with differing consequences. This positioning influences whether their voice(s) are heard by those with relatively more power. As has been clearly documented, social work, a largely feminised occupation, has never achieved the sort of professional closure and status that other, largely masculinised, occupations have (Hugman 1991). In the process social work has struggled, and continues to struggle, to have anything approaching a credible 'voice'. Whether this is due to social work's inherent failure to adequately address challenges and criticisms, to the satisfaction of the wider public and politicians, or the impact of wider structuring systems that shape and limit social work responses, is open to question. Just as it is open to question whether those parents who 'fail' to care and protect their children do so as a result of their 'individual pathology' or the impact of wider oppressive and divisive structures that shape all our experiences in differing ways (e.g. Davies, 1985; Dale *et al.*, 1986; Frost and Stern, 1989). Assessments made of social work credibility, either at the micro level in terms of individual social work practice, or at the macro level, in terms of collective social work responses, will reflect more than just the 'objective' judgements that seek to understand the 'facts'. All responses are situated. Specific articulations of our understanding of complex social issues are based on acceptance of particular moral, political, economic, and social 'truths'. With that in mind it seems appropriate to clearly state that this chapter unashamedly attempts to challenge the potentially dominant narrative of social work incompetence – even as we acknowledge that there is always room to improve practice in any professional arena. This position follows ongoing contact with many social workers and managers, both through the research undertaken for my post-graduate work and my ongoing friendships with people who are still in practice, who continue to work with the contradictions and tensions of protecting children and supporting families in difficult circumstances. Their 'good enough', and at times exceptional, practice often passes unnoticed and unacknowledged.

Themes generated
As staff, at all levels within Northtown, attempted to explain the nature of their work with children and their families a range of core issues emerged. The following represents a summary of some of the main concerns raised as staff assessed and tried to explain the extent to which the legislation had or had not been implemented in their authority despite the best intentions of both managers and practitioners.

- Financial concerns were important for all staff. This is unsurprising as the local council was facing severe financial difficulties that led to a 10% reduction in the budget for social services in the year 1996/ 1997 (when the main fieldwork was undertaken). This followed previous financial restraint, in 1996/1995, as the council implemented strategies to avoid overspend– for example, delay in filling vacancies for as long as possible. In addition, permanent reductions were to be identified in the financial year 1997/1998 that would also impact on the nature of service provision. The extent to which these issues were *the* reason or *a* reason for problems in practice was the source of debate and disagreement amongst staff. Managers were less likely than front-line staff to attribute all problems to budgetary restraint.

● Importation of changing management practices and the rise of a 'business culture', focused on the centrality of 'value for money', were key issues as managers attempted to balance the books and reassure local councillors that they were doing everything possible to stay within budget restrictions. This led to conflict between differing groups as front-line staff increasingly believed that decisions were not taken on the basis of knowledge of good practice, and the requirements of the legislation, but rather on the need to 'save money'. Prioritising resource distribution and making 'tough' decisions were a key management task which staff interpreted as an increasing concern with figures not people. In this environment adversarial relationships were evident across the occupational hierarchy, as mistrust and conflict were becoming endemic within an authority that had enjoyed largely positive management/staff relations in the past. Within this context the pivotal role occupied by team leaders, as they mediate relationships between front-line staff and managers, was becoming increasingly stressful as individuals attempted to bridge what was seen as a widening gap.

● Organisational restructuring at differing levels had been, and was being, undertaken. Corporate restructuring was near completion, to meet central government agendas around the provision of 'seamless' services to citizen consumers, and this had led to the development of a new department – Community Services – by the chief executive and management board. This followed more local restructuring as social service managers had attempted to configure services to meet the demands of the NHS and Community Care Act 1990 – through separation of children and families from adult services and the establishment of a 'soft' purchaser/provider split in the former. Further changes were being discussed in an attempt to restructure the children and families division to ensure resources were 'used appropriately' to provide effective service responses.

- Increasing proceduralisation and standardisation were evident as staff had to accommodate wide-sweeping changes to policies and procedures including: increasing centralisation of decision making, greater prescription around appropriate social work interventions, a move to specialisation within and across teams, and the redefining of threshold criteria when assessing the need for services with any child and family. Most staff believed these changes led to more bureaucracy not the development of better services.

- Redefinition of roles and responsibilities as field staff were increasingly involved in child protection-focused interventions as other staff – for example, day centre workers – had to deal with role expansion as their job descriptions were renegotiated to reflect changing organisational needs.

Although staff at all levels were committed to the values, ideas, and focus of the Children Act 1989 there were clearly many problems in practice that inhibited them as they tried to work within the spirit of the Act. For example, despite the authority's attempt to 'hear' and incorporate Messages from Research (DoH 1995), through assessment and potential 'refocusing' of service responses, staff believed that coercive child-protection-focused interventions were increasingly the norm within the division. In the process, supportive family-centred practice was being eroded – despite the best attempts of managers and staff to resist this trend and the evidence of prior 'good practice' of support work with families within the authority. For many the fear that the organisation would be left with nothing other than the 'rump of child protection work' – which many staff did not want to engage with as a primary aspect of their practice – was ever present in Northtown. This despite widespread acknowledgement, by the majority of staff, that it was antithetical to the intentions enshrined in the Children Act 1989 and out of step with government rhetoric regarding the importance of ensuring that children in need receive adequate service responses from local authority departments.

Ultimately, all staff, to varying extents, felt their working environment had been destabilised in ways that inhibited their best attempts to provide responsive, child- and family-centred interventions to those requesting, or being directed to, services. As staff said:

It is increasingly chaotic

Qualified field social worker

... people are so punch drunk with change they find it difficult to take things on board... the great thing is we are reorganising, we're cutting our budgets and at the same time we are expected as children and families teams to take on board new documents . . . guidelines policies/ procedures... there's that much going on that people are kind of in a spin
Qualified field social worker

Overall, there was a sense that what had been a relatively stable organisation, for example evidenced by low rates of sickness and staff turnover, was becoming an increasingly 'incoherent'[7] organisation. In this context the majority of staff and some managers were struggling to cope with the contradictory, chaotic and contentious expectations of work in a statutory setting in the 1990s as external agendas exerted a range of pressures that could not be resisted but had to be accommodated. Finally, I shall end this section with a quote, so staff have the 'last word'. Many staff wanted to 'be given the tools to do the job' so they could 'lift a finger' to help those who are 'loaded up' in our society and often 'blamed for failing'. Without this the majority of staff felt fairly pessimistic about the future:

. . . and there is a professional impact and a personal one and some overlap between the two . . . if you are coming in to do a job and you recognise that a job needs doing and your management tells you to do a job but they are not giving you the tools to do it . . . that is a recipe for frustration but when there is no acknowledgement that they are not giving you the tools and the expectation is there that you do the job then that is a recipe for frustration, anger, and enormous stress . . . and in some ways that dynamic is there for managers in relation to politicians . . . but I can't let myself feel too sorry for them... and everybody knows you need supportive teams and supportive management in this line of work to survive it . . . well people are beginning to stop . . . there have been people crying at their desks lately . . . and so many people trying to leave . . . get jobs outside the local authority . . . take early retirement . . . what does that tell you?
Qualified Social Worker 4(F)

Discussion

Social work with children and families – like social work more generally – is inevitably, probably terminally, contentious. The search for the modernist Holy Grail of the perfect system, to ensure children are protected and parents supported, cannot but end in failure. The contemporary history of child care practice, like more distant history, is fraught with tensions as agendas shift and agreement, as to solutions, eludes us. Recent research and theorising have highlighted some consensus, in terms of the belief that change in the child care arena is needed, yet there is no agreement as to the way forward (Gibbons 1995). For example, some writers argue we need to more clearly separate out the care and control functions and locate child protection work outside social services (Parton 1995b), whilst others argue that we need to reconfigure services within statutory agencies to more clearly delineate differing aspects of provision (Bamford 1990). Ultimately, there isn't a single solution to the question of how we can best ensure that children generally, and those who have contact with state-sponsored agencies specifically, reach adulthood as unscathed by their formative experiences, within a highly divisive and divided society, as is possible. As Walby (1998) states, when discussing the findings of The National Commission of Inquiry into the prevention of child abuse:

> *The facts and evidence presented to the commission led to the inescapable conclusion that the present high social and political tolerance of the suffering of children, through inadequate or actively detrimental policies and provisions, has a direct bearing upon what we now commonly call child abuse* (p. 83).

In addition, as many authors have highlighted, lessons learnt are also often lessons forgotten in the history of child care policy and practice (e.g. Walby 1998). Discussion of problems and responses has a sort of circular quality in that many difficulties, and proposed solutions to identified problems, have been debated before as legislative and organisational shifts have been formulated and implemented (Holman 1998; Hughes 1998). On some levels the problems are insoluble within a society, and arguably a world, so structured by inequality that our whole lives, from cradle to grave, are filtered through our experiences of material and cultural advantage or disadvantage. Having said that, and not wishing to succumb to despair, there are clearly more or less empowering and enabling ways to deliver services to children at risk of harm from their parents, or families at risk of harm within an inherently unequal society. For example, operating to a normative model, that attempts to judge situated and specific concerns without recourse to deterministic, formulaic, and individualistic analysis alone, may offer us an appropriate framework for judging claims around what is, or is not, acceptable child care practice or responses to problems in practice. As Parton *et al.*, (1997) state:

> *Notions of ambiguity, complexity and uncertainty are the core of social work and should be built upon not defined out (p.23).*

However, to operate to such a normative – rather than the arguably dominant individualistic, medical – model to understand the difficulties some children face in their families requires that we defend such assertions in practice. Embedded within claims, and counter-claims, about appropriate ways to work with children and families are beliefs about what can be characterised as reasonable and reasoned professional responses. As Munro (1998) states, we have to find ways to judge between competing claims at the micro level, when assessing the need for interventions with particular children and their families, and at the macro level, when considering which theories for practice are more or less defensible in practice. This is clearly not easy and social work has arguably had great difficulty assertively articulating a credible basis for child care practice.

Against this backdrop the role for state employees, who are empowered and entrusted with the responsibility of mediating the relationship between the child, family, and state, cannot but be the subject of intense and contradictory debate. Unfortunately, and again predictably, some voices dominate that debate whilst others are drowned out. In general, it is possible to argue that the construction of narratives about social work has largely failed to give voice to social workers' experiences, as workers, as they attempt to provide services to vulnerable members of society. Whilst it is important that there is space to hear critiques of social work theorising and practice, it is also imperative that counter-narratives are constructed and articulated that serve to question, and probably challenge, what might be seen as the dominant narrative around the role and task for contemporary social work. As Rojek *et al.*, (1988) stated, society 'harbours profound doubts' about the value of social work even as social workers struggle to

> *reconcile interests which may be objectively irreconcilable and produce solutions for social problems which exist in a molten change-able condition* (p.175).

It seems inevitable in this context that moral panics about social work practice will appear on a regular basis as problems are highlighted around specific individuals, for example Kimberley Carlisle, or groups, such as parents with drug or alcohol problems, or in particular locations, for example Cleveland. Ultimately, again as Rojek *et al.*, (1988) state:

The ease and fluency with which most panics against social work swing into action in the media suggest the existence of a deep reservoir of negative energy in the public's mind against social work (p.151).

Although there is clearly a need to recognise and deal with instances of poor social work practice we must also de-construct and re-construct narratives to document the difficulties of contemporary practice as social workers struggle with the tensions of providing services to clients 'in the margins'. As academics and politicians consider and debate ways forward, staff within agencies, like families within wider society, struggle with the contradictions and tensions of their lived experiences in difficult circumstances. Re-constructive theorising is needed if staff are not to be disempowered and overwhelmed by assertions about social work incompetence that continue to dominate much contemporary debate. As Parton *et al.*, (1997) state, children and families social work takes place in a contradictory context as political, economic, legal, and social agendas change and the task for social work is defined and re-defined – often in confusing ways. For example, even as social workers are increasingly exhorted to focus on supporting families, as their primary mandate, they are also required to respond to the increasing number of child protection allegations that necessitate a focus on investigating and policing families. In addition, as Ball (1998) states, local authorities have had to deal with burgeoning statutory responsibilities even as greater controls have been imposed to regulate the discretionary exercise of statutory powers. More specifically, the exercise of social workers' professional judgements has been circumscribed by changing organisation and management practices – particularly the rise to dominance of managerialist principles and practice.

Concluding comments

This chapter attempts to offer support to the muted narrative of social work competence, without recourse to deterministic theorising, even as I recognise that differing versions of that narrative co-exist. Offering a challenge to the playing down of social work achievements, even as failures are consistently highlighted in ways that they are not for other professional groups, is necessary if we are interested in challenging the scapegoating of many committed, conscientious, and hard-working professionals within state-sponsored agencies. Clearly, there are no easy answers to questions about the 'way forward' – there are just varied visions of the future. These visions will inform construction of a framework within which more- or less-enabling responses to clients can be delivered – even as staff struggle with the contradictions of practice. A key question must then be whose agenda, as change is negotiated or imposed, will dominate and determine policy and practice in the near and distant future. As authors in Parton's (1997) edited collection highlight, we need to consider what is to become of social work, alternatively stated to think about its futures, even as we recognise there is no one way forward. More specifically, as Langan and Clarke (1994) state, visions of the future may be more- or less-optimistic or pessimistic as staff struggle to provide services in confusing, problematic, and largely crisis-ridden contexts. If we look through an optimist's lens, change may be viewed as a route to improve services for clients. However, through a pessimist's lens we might argue that recent changes have led to the systematic destabilisation of erstwhile functioning organisations as particular political agendas have been implemented. In either case, staff within social service departments have had to contend with profound material and cultural change in the recent past which is likely to continue into the future. In the process they have had to deal with the cognitive dissonance and stress generated as they struggle with the contradictions of practice within under-funded and dangerously overloaded social service departments (Seebohm, 1989; NALGO, 1990; Schorr, 1991; La Velle and Lyons, 1996a; 1996b).

Social work interventions, like family functioning, need situating within the wider socio-economic and political context which frame them if we are not to succumb to hostile, negative, and largely simplistic analysis of professional interventions. Social workers, like many parents, need support to meet the requirements of their role. However, they, like many of those who use services, may be casualties not survivors of recent, or future, changes. Let's wait and see what happens as the new political administration reconfigures services and attempts to redefine organisational, and professional, roles and responsibilities. Whether the current political administration will make good on its commitment to support staff (e.g. DoH 1998d; DoH 1999d) in their respective roles remains to be seen. That ongoing debate and critical analysis are needed cannot be denied. Hopefully we can ensure the full range of 'voices' are heard as we debate agendas and attempt to reformulate or formulate responses as we seek to offer responsive services to children and their families.

Appendix
The empirical basis for this chapter
The theoretical reflections contained in this chapter are rooted in research undertaken within one small metropolitan social services department between 1995 and 1998 – here called Northtown[8]. This organisational case-

study provided an empirical resource for the creative and structured investigation of staff perceptions of the extent to which legislative and policy changes, the Children Act 1989 and NHS and Community Care Act 1990, had been implemented within children and families services. Wider structural and historical issues were explored with reference to the lived experiences of work with the contradictions of contemporary practice as the nature, as well as the impact and consequences, of any changes from a service provider perspective was documented and analysed.

In general, a participatory approach was taken to the research production process – for example, through use of focus groups at the beginning of the research cycle to facilitate staff input into the formulation of the interview guide. However, recognition of the limitations to full participation, personal and organisational, was clearly evident. For example, feedback of preliminary results and review of findings with staff was postponed due to researcher ill health. When this aspect of the research cycle was finally operationalised, several months after it should have been, no organisational members participated in the planned sessions. Clearly, this had an impact in terms of the extent to which staff were able to comment on, and possibly challenge, the researchers' analysis of the data. More specifically, the collection of data for analysis focused on two distinct sources of information:

- Organisational products, documents, and statistics, 'objective' evidence of the work of the department or non-reactive reference points (Morgan, 1988).

- Perceptions of organisational members, 'subjective' evidence of the work of the department (Morgan, 1988).

And occurred in three distinct phases:

- Initial fieldwork – meetings with key organisational personnel, focus group discussions (4), pilot interviews (6) and collection of some organisational products.

- Main fieldwork – interviews across the hierarchy[9] (34), specific meeting attendance and final collection of organisational products (40+).

- Final fieldwork – feedback of analysis and discussion with participants through attendance at the Children's Services Management group meeting and focus group discussions (2).

Throughout the process there was an attempt to balance a focus on structural concerns, inter-personal and intra-personal issues, whilst undertaking a systematic and intuitive analysis. Time to reflect, make connections, and question formulations-facilitated work with the ambiguities and tensions evident across accounts, whilst looking for themes or exceptions and telling the 'story'.

Notes

1. A note on authorship. Situating the 'self' as a social researcher is increasingly recognised as a route to greater transparency – as the reader may get some sense of the person behind the analysis. The inclusion of remote and current biographical (Lofland and Lofland, 1984) or autobiographical (Stanley, 1986) material is then an integral part of the production process – not a peripheral or egoistic concern. However, selection of personal biographical material, applicable to any work in hand, is undoubtedly idiosyncratic and difficult to deliver in a meaningful way – not least as we decide what it is relevant for others to know about us as people when occupying what are essentially professional roles. In the process we inevitably edit our complex social identities and select what is worthy of note. In academic terms this clearly links to the way in which we want others to 'read' our analysis, presenting biographical details does some work for us. With these caveats in mind I should like to document my experience as a social worker – as this seems relevant in this context. After qualifying – having completed the BA (Hons.) Social Work at Lancaster University – I worked in a client reception team in Bolton, a Family Service Unit, and for the NSPCC. My most recent contact with staff in social service departments has been through my postgraduate research, whilst a student at the University of Central Lancashire, and my current employment as a lecturer in the Directorate of Social Work and Social Care at the University of Salford.

2. This chapter focuses on the role for state-sponsored employees working as social workers, or social work managers, with children and their families within local authority departments. To avoid repetition all references to social work are taken to mean this particular group of social workers, unless otherwise stated. Such differentiation is arguably increasingly important on two counts. First, post-modern concerns sensitise us to the extent to which totalising theorising fails to recognise the differences that exist between those situated in specific ways in any society. Second, and more pragmatically, recent organisation and management shifts have positioned those employed as social workers in very different ways across the public, voluntary, and private sectors.

3. As Murphy (1996) highlights, the periodic symbolic, or actual, sacrifice of a human 'scapegoat' fulfils an important social function for others. In the childcare social work arena the ritualised sacrifice of social workers, for example by the media when another 'scandal' erupts, may well serve to protect others, politicians/the public, from honest exploration of their roles in the ongoing abuse of some children by adults. Even as social workers manage moral risks (Hollis and Howe 1987), as they are involved in complex and contradictory decision making that inevitably involves intangible elements that avoid easy schematisation, they hold some of the contradictions of contemporary living for the public and politicians alike. If we are a 'civilised' society, as many would like to believe, we need to explain 'uncivilised' behaviour – and child abuse, especially sexual abuse, is just that. If we can routinely scapegoat social workers for their 'failure' to protect we may well avoid wider societal exploration of our corporate adult responsibility for the negative and damaging experiences that many children

continue to suffer in our civilised society.

4. There are clearly a number of terms in current use, which are used to describe those who use state-sponsored welfare services. Although other writers, for example Hadley and Clough (1996), have rejected the use of 'client', as they argue it has connotations of dependence that are unhelpful in the contemporary context, this is problematic from my perspective. Use of the label 'service user' has been said to be least offensive, as it does not reflect the narrow focus on market relationships implied by the term 'consumer' (Hadley and Clough, 1996). However, it is possible to argue that this still denies and minimises differences between the State and the market as mechanisms to provide services to people in need in unacceptable ways. Whether the current government wishes us to believe that social services provision is for 'all' (DoH 1998a), rather than for the residuum that cannot provide for themselves within a capitalist economy, the reality remains that most of those who use social services provision are those with limited or no access to other forms of provision. Social services departments, unlike education and health, continue to largely offer services to a specific sub-section of the population. Changing the language, without more-fundamental changes to the organisation of welfare, is confusing at best and potentially offensive at worst.

5. The Appendix offers a summary of the empirical basis for this chapter.

6. As Lyman (1995) states the term 'new social movements' can be applied in differing ways by social commentators. In this instance it is used to describe a range of political challenges that have been organised around specific interests – for example, ecological concerns.

7. As Hadley and Clough (1996) make clear, when discussing adult services, changes in the welfare arena, particularly the importation of market principles and the rise to dominance of managerial and/or political priorities, have resulted in changing organisational forms. They argue that this has led to the evolution of new organisations that can be characterised as either coherent or incoherent. Incoherent organisations are those in disarray verging on chaos. Within these organisations the principal agenda is the solution of financial problems as bureaucracy proliferates and services are increasingly focused on minimal provision for those most in 'need'. Defence and delay are evident at the organisational level whilst staff continue to try to provide services to clients despite the emergence of organisational blocks to this in practice. In these environments confusion and defensiveness are endemic as a desperate search for survival, rather than planned and coherent initiatives, drives change. In this framework staff are increasingly demoralised, devalued, and frustrated. Finally, low job-satisfaction, constrained autonomy, problematic role changes, and increasingly difficult communication between managers and staff are evident as the contradictions of practice threaten to overwhelm personnel.

8. Some basic background information will be provided about the host site for the research – to facilitate the reader's sense of place and to provide some point of potential comparison for others working in the statutory sector. Northtown is a metropolitan borough with a population of approximately 300,000. There are clear contrasts within the authority, as evidenced by measures of deprivation and health trends. Examination of the index of local deprivation for local authorities (Department of Environment, Transport and Regions 1998) indicates that Northtown is well positioned generally, despite wide variations across the borough, in comparison with other local metropolitan boroughs. This index scores authorities across variables with negative scores indicating what they term non-deprived values and positive values indicating increasing deprivation. Against this index Northtown is positioned on the scale with authorities like Eastbourne, Oxford, and Richmond. Alternatively stated the range is 0-40.07 and

Northtown falls in the 50th percentile.

9. When negotiating formal access it was agreed that some staff groups that provided services to children and their families would be excluded from the research – for example, youth justice workers. The rationale for any exclusion was linked either to organisational issues or theoretical concerns – for example, the differing focus of work within the youth justice team. Once the categories for inclusion in the study had been agreed, personnel supplied me with staff lists. A vertical slice was then taken across the occupational hierarchy and people were allocated to one of four occupational categories. These were: higher managers; front line managers; qualified social workers (this included those occupying posts that require a social work qualification); unqualified social workers (this included those occupying posts which can be categorised as offering a social work service but without requiring a social work qualification). This approach reflects others' categorisation of individuals and/or groups when undertaking research within social work agencies (Hadley and Hugman 1988; Balloch *et al.*, 1995). This practical strategy links to theoretical concerns – for example, feminist and postmodern – around the need to capture the multiplicity of voices rather than merely generating a 'story' that is likely to reflect the dominant discourse (Plummer, 1995).

References

Ball, C (1998) 'Regulating child care: from the Children Act 1948 to the present day' *Child and Family Social Work* 3(3), pp 163-172

Balloch, S, Andre, T, Ginn, J, McLean, J and Williams, J (1995) *Working in the Social Services* London, NISW

Bamford, T (1990) *The Future of Social Work* London, Macmillan

Beresford, P and Croft, S (1986) *Whose Welfare?. Private Care and Public Services* Brighton, The Lewis Cohen Urban Studies Centre

Cleaver, H and Freeman, P (1995) *Parental Perspectives in Cases of Suspected Child Abuse* London, HMSO

Cleaver, H, Wattam, C and Cawson, P (1998) *Assessing Risk in Child Protection* London, NSPCC

Dale, P, Davies, M, Morrison, T and Waters, J (1986) *Dangerous Families* London, Routledge

Davies, M (1985) *The Essential Social Worker. A Guide to Practice* Aldershot, Wildwood Ltd

Department of the Environment, Transport and the Regions (1998) *Index of Local Deprivation – Local Authority Scores and Values on 12 Indicators* http: //www. regeneration.detr.gov.uk/98ild/index.html

Department of Health (1995) *Child Protection: Messages from Research. Studies in Child Protection* London, HMSO

Department of Health (1997) *Social Services – Achievement and Challenge*

London, HMSO

Department of Health (1998a) *Modernising Social Services. Promoting Independence. Improving Protection. Raising Standards* London, The Stationery Office

Department of Health (21.10.98b) *Health secretary pledges to transform children's services* http://www.nds.coi.gov.uk/coi/coipres – accessed 20/5/1999.

Department of Health (1998c) *Draft Guidance sets out new plans to fight child abuse* http://www.nds.coi.gov.uk/coi/coipre – accessed 20/5/1999.

Department of Health (18.11.98d) *Social services training to get extra 20 million http://www.nds.coi.gov.uk/coi/coipre* – accessed 20.5.99.

Department of Health (23.2.99a) *Performance tables for social services to be introduced* http://www.nds.coi.gov.uk/coi/coipre – accessed 20/5/1999.

Department of Health (11.2.99b) *Councillors have crucial role in improving services to children* http://www.nds.coi.gov.uk./coi/coipre – accessed 20/5/1999.

Department of Health (21.4.99d) *Action to be taken to protect social service staff. National summit to take place this autumn to develop strategy* http://www.nds.coi.gov.uk/coi/coipr – accessed 20.5.99.

Foren, R and Bailey, R (1968) *Authority in Social Casework* London, Pergamon Press

Frost, N and Stern, M (1989) *The Politics of Child Welfare* London, Harvester Wheatsheaf

Gibbons, J (1995) 'The Child Protection System: Objectives and Evaluation' in *Rethinking Child Protection. Research Leading the Way* Lancaster, Lancaster University Conference Papers

Hadley, R and Clough, R (1996) *Care in Chaos. Frustration and Challenge in Community Care* Cambridge, Cassell

Hadley, R and Hugman, R (1988) *Evaluating Change in Stockport Social Services. The Baseline 1988* Department of Social Administration, University of Lancaster, Lancaster

Handler, J (1968) 'The Coercive Children's Officer' *New Society* 3 October, pp 485-87

Hollis, M and Howe, D (1987) 'Moral Risks in Social Work' *Journal of*

Applied Philosophy 4(2), pp 123-33

Holman, B (1993) *A New Deal for Social Welfare* Oxford, Lion Books

Holman, B (1998) 'From Children's Departments to Family Departments' *Child and Family Social Work* 3(3), pp 205-11

Hudson, B (1993) 'Michael Lipsky and Street Level Bureaucracy' in Hill, M (ed.) *The Policy Process. A Reader* London, Harvester Wheatsheaf

Hughes, R (1998) 'Children Act 1948 and 1989: similarities, differences, continuities' *Child and Family Social Work* 3(3), pp 149-52

Hugman, R (1991) *Power in the Caring Professions* London, MacMillan, London

Hugman, R and Smith, D (1995) 'Ethical issues in social work: an overview' in Hugman, R and Smith, D (eds) *Ethical Issues in Social Work* London, Routledge

Jacques, M (1998) 'Good to be Back' *Marxism Today* Nov/Dec, pp 2-3

James, A (1994) *Managing to Care* London, Longman

Jones, C and Novak, T (1993) 'Social work Today' *British Journal of Social Work* 23 pp 195-212

Langan, M and Clarke, J (1994) 'Managing in the Mixed economy of Care' in Clarke, J, Cochrane, A and McLaughlin, E (eds) *Managing Social Policy* London, Sage

La Velle, I and Lyons, K (1996a) 'The Social Worker Speaks: I – perceptions of recent changes in British social work' *Practice* 8(2), pp 25-30

La Velle, I and Lyons, K (1996b) 'The Social Worker Speaks: II – management of change in the personal social services' *Practice* 8(3), pp 63-71

Lofland, J and Lofland, L (1984) *Analyzing Social Settings* (2nd ed.) Belmont, Wadsworth Publishing

Lyman, S (1995) 'Introduction' in Lyman, S (ed.) *Social Movements. Critiques, Concepts, Case-Studies* London, Macmillan, London

Morgan, D (1988) *Focus Groups as Qualitative Research* London, Sage

Munro, E (1998) *Understanding Social Work. An Empirical Approach* London, Athlone Press

Murphy, T (1996) *Rethinking the War on Drugs in Ireland* Cork, Cork

University Press

Murray, C (1994) *Underclass; The Crisis Deepens* London, IEA

NALGO (1990) *Social Work in Crisis. A Study of Conditions in Six Local Authorities* London, NALGO

Packman, J and Jordan, B (1991) 'The Children Act: Looking Forward, Looking Back' *British Journal of Social Work* 21, 315-27

Parton, N (1995a) *Governing the Family. Childcare, Child Protection and the State* London, Macmillan

Parton, N (1995b) 'Child Welfare and Policing' in *Rethinking Child Protection. Research Leading the Way* Lancaster, Lancaster University Conference Papers

Parton, N (1997) *Child Protection and Family Support: Tensions, contradictions and possibilities* London, Routledge

Parton, N, Thorpe, D and Wattam, C (1997) *Child Protection and Family Support. Risk and the moral Order* London, Routledge

Payne, M (1991) *Modern Social Work Theory: A Critical Introduction* London, Macmillan

Plummer, K (1995) *Telling Sexual Stories* London, Routledge

Richards, M, Payne, M and Sheppard, A (1990) *Staff Supervision in Child Protection Work* London, NISW

Rojek, C, Peacock, G and Collins, S (1988) *Social Work and Received Ideas* London, Routledge

Satyamurti, C (1981) *Occupational Survival* London, Basil Blackwell

Schorr, A (1992) *The Personal Social Services: An Outside View* York, Joseph Rowntree Foundation

Seebohm, F (1989) *Seebohm Twenty years on: Three Stages in the Development of the Personal Social Services* Exeter, Policy Studies Institute

Stanley, L. (1986) 'Some Thoughts on Editing the Diaries of Hannah Cullwick' *Feminist Research Seminar – Feminist Research Process, Studies in Sexual Politics 16* Sociology Department, University of Manchester

Walby, C (1998) 'The National Commission of Inquiry into the prevention of child abuse: will it make a difference' *Child Abuse Review* 7(2), pp 77-86

Wise, S (1991) Manchester, Sociology Department, Manchester

Metropolitan Monograph Series